Antarctic Sketchbook

Best wishes Claudia

Claudia Myatt

Published in 2023 by Golden Duck (UK) Ltd.
Sokens, Green Street, Pleshey, near Chelmsford,
Essex, CM3 1HT
golden-duck.co.uk

Written by Claudia Myatt

Illustrated by Claudia Myatt

Typeset by Bertie Wheen

Printed by Biddles Books Ltd
biddles.co.uk

ISBN 978-1-899262-61-8

claudiamyatt.co.uk

CONTENTS

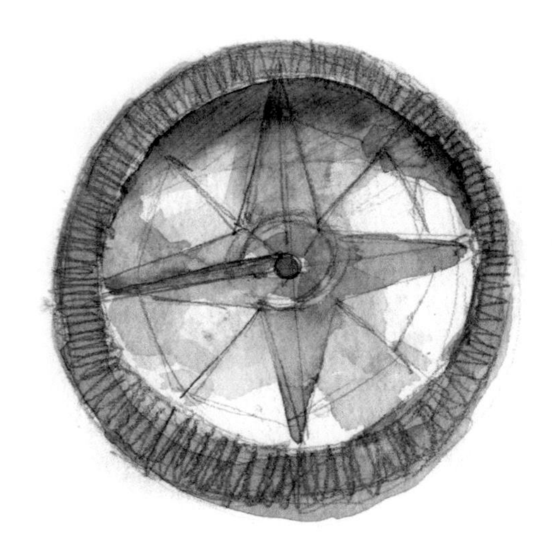

Praise for *Antarctic Sketchbook*

'Claudia Myatt's Antarctic Sketchbook *offers a vivid impression of the terrain, the weather, the flora and fauna of this unique and remote part of our world. And above all, the 'feel' of it, captured in words and brief, vivid watercolour sketches. "It's as if the atmosphere is thinner (perhaps it is)," she writes, "but each breath you take makes you feel you haven't been breathing properly for years." [...] It truly feeds the fascination many of us have with the Antarctic.'*

Peter Willis, review for *Yachting Monthly* magazine

'Antarctica and South Georgia are places that makes you want to burst with gratitude and excitement – Claudia sparkles off the seas in her latest multi-dimensional book. It's a gripping account for sailors, artists and explorers of our times. Each page shows an explosion of Claudia's lively interest, creative viewpoints, freedom, wit and thoughts in watercolour sketches and writing.

Her voyage to Antarctica as artist in residence gave her long days of contemplation and observation in isolation and at sea. She describes the workings and personalities of a research ship and the crew's initial astonishment at her sketches. She meets wildlife and people, and distant land masses. She greets past and present at the old whaling station at Grytviken and she relishes in the silence of the high latitudes, the deep south and the Antarctic peninsula. Claudia's thirst for the unknown is almost saturated by the blues of her palette. Antarctic Sketchbook *is a book to explore our time as well as an adventure into the waves and the blues of the ice, snow and sea.*

It's her best yet.'

Mary Anne Bartlett, Art Safari & Close Encounters Travel

'Claudia Myatt's new book, Antarctic Sketchbook*, captivated me immediately. Her sketches are so alive and perfectly reflect her narrative. I felt I was with her throughout the voyage. A must for any sailor or anyone with a lust for adventure.'*

Jim Wyllie, author of *Cedric the Seahorse* series

'I very much like its variety of techniques and mediums on one page...monochrome and colour, texts, lists, painting, drawing. I love the icy palette and the way she paints cold with such economy, ie approaching Thule, the Presence of Cold, Horseshoe I. (And in the last I like the comforting cupboard with its tins against the forbidding image of sea and rock). My favourite is a very simple, ice-cold one called 17th Dec. I also like the red boats, Viola, *Leaving Harbour and the bold red shape in HMS* Protector. *And not forgetting the figures, some very strong images of people in their kit...Frank Debenham (plus mustard!) and the girl in Helly Hansen gear. And I admire the contrast in scale of figures dwarfed by huge rocks as in BAS station Orkneys.'*

Susie Hamilton, artist and daughter of polar explorer Augustine Courtauld

Acknowledgements

Heartfelt thanks to the Friends of Scott Polar Research Institute for having the vision to create the Artist in Residence opportunities. It is a privilege to be able to share my own impressions of a very special place.

Thank you to the Royal Navy for your hospitality; to Captain Michael Wood and his crew who made me welcome on board HMS *Protector*, took the trouble to make sure I had everything I needed and had the opportunity to go ashore. It was fascinating to witness first hand the important work that is being done by the ship in surveying and helping to ensure that Antarctica has the protection and care that it needs.

Thank you to my editor, friend and mentor Julia Jones of Golden Duck Publishing who gives so much of her time in gently coaxing my words into better shape.

About the Author

Claudia Myatt is a maritime illustrator, artist and writer. She likes to spend as much time as possible at sea or up a creek, sketching in quiet places. She is the author/illustrator of the *Go Sailing!* series of books for the Royal Yachting Association as well as *Sketchbook Sailor*, *One Line at a Time*, *Anglo-Saxon Inspirations* and *Keeping a Sketchbook Diary* for Golden Duck Publications. She lives afloat on the River Deben in Suffolk. Hobbies include kayaking, sailing, drinking wine and playing Celtic harp (but not all at once).

And if anyone knows a ship going south that needs an artist, let her know – there are plenty of sketchbooks yet to be filled!

www.claudiamyatt.co.uk
facebook: Claudia Myatt Illustration
instagram: myattclaudia

Other Titles by Claudia Myatt from Golden Duck

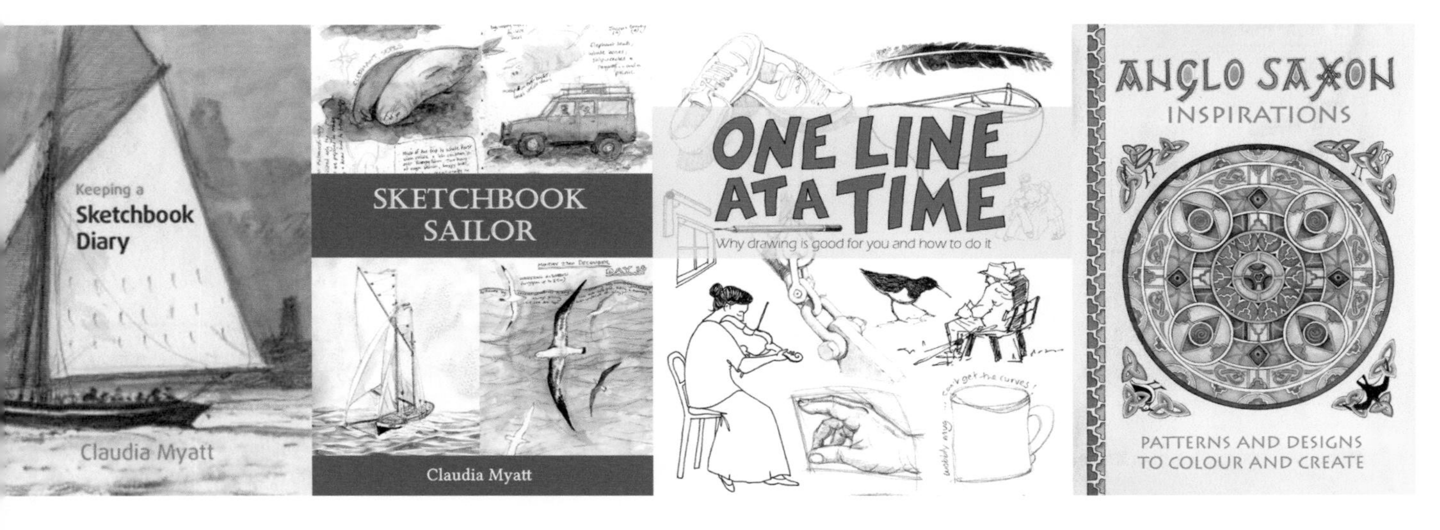

We also hold most titles in Claudia Myatt's RYA *Go Sailing!* series.

FOREWORD

It is my great pleasure to write this Foreword for *Antarctic Sketchbook* by Claudia Myatt.

At the end of November 2020, Claudia was selected by the Friends of the Scott Polar Research Institute to be our Artist in Residence and given the opportunity to fulfil a lifetime's dream and visit Antarctica onboard the Royal Navy ice patrol ship – HMS *Protector*. But the global impact of the COVID-19 pandemic meant her trip south had to be postponed. It was to be a year later in November 2021 before she finally joined the ship.

Although Claudia is a marine artist and an experienced sailor, this was her first time on a Royal Navy ship and her first visit to Antarctica. But she was not daunted by the five-week voyage onboard HMS *Protector* and embraced the adventure. She used her sketchbooks as a journal charting her incredible voyage from the Falkland Islands to South Georgia, and then to the remote South Sandwich Islands, and finally to the Antarctic Peninsula. She returned home to Suffolk with three sketchbooks jammed full of her watercolour paintings of the waves and sea, polar landscapes, wildlife, the ship and her crew.

I would like to thank the Royal Navy for their great support for Claudia. She was very well looked after on HMS *Protector* and her Commanding Officer – Captain Michael Wood MBE – and crew gave her a fascinating insight into their important work patrolling and surveying the Antarctic and South Atlantic.

It is wonderful to see that her paintings and her story have now been published in *Antarctic Sketchbook*. I hope you enjoy the book!

John Shears

Dr John Shears
Chairman of the Friends of the Scott Polar Research Institute
15 September 2023

PREFACE

'I hope you don't mind me asking,' said the young marine commando, 'but what are you doing here?'

The three marines from HMS *Protector* were sharing their tot of whisky with me at the Shackleton memorial in South Georgia. At the foot of the stone cross a fur seal dozed gently and the cold wind whipped the pages of my sketchbook making the wet colours blend into a puddle.

It was a good question – what on earth was a woman old enough to be their grandmother doing on a working Navy ship with her sketchbook and paints? I told them the easy answer first, that I was this year's Artist in Residence appointed by Friends of Scott Polar Research Institute. Their question, though, deserved more of an answer. What they were really asking is, why have an artist at all? What's the point?

It's about communication, I said. Using art to appeal to people who may never have the chance to come here, why places like South Georgia, the Southern Ocean and Antarctica are important as well as beautiful. Sketches, paintings, songs and stories bring faraway places closer. They nourish the imagination, reflect the past as well as the present and make the world a bigger and more interesting place.

Maybe my sketchbooks and what I do with them will inspire a few others to start drawing too, enriching their own lives. After an extraordinary trip I came home with three full sketchbooks, each page a swirl of lines and colours evoking memories of ice, glaciers, mountains, wildlife, people, history, life on board ship, sea, sky and birds. I tried to draw not just what I was seeing but what I was feeling, and what it is about the Antarctic air and landscape that makes you feel more intensely alive.

snow petrel

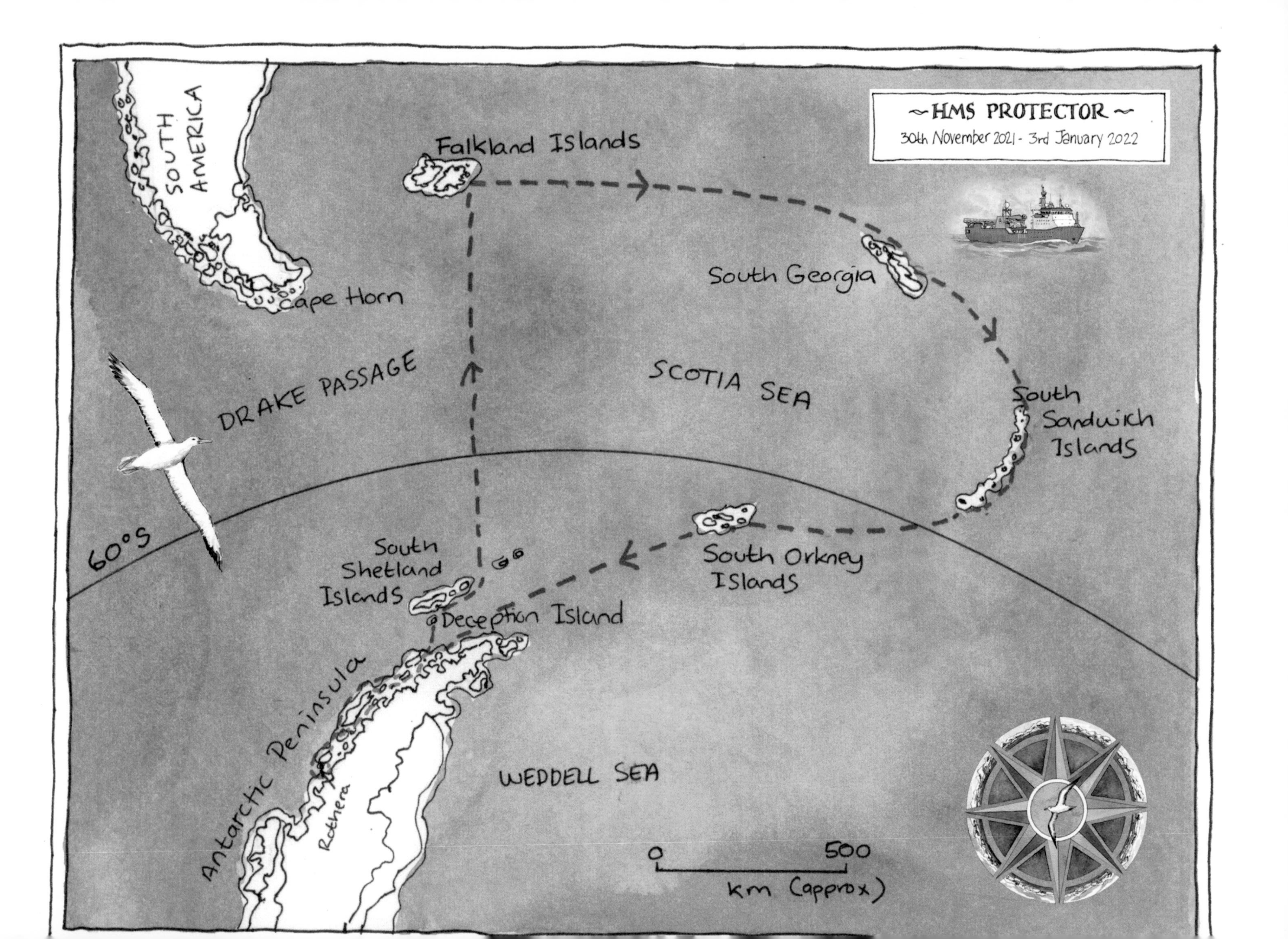
~ HMS PROTECTOR ~
30th November 2021 - 3rd January 2022
SOUTH AMERICA
Falkland Islands
Cape Horn
South Georgia
DRAKE PASSAGE
SCOTIA SEA
South Sandwich Islands
60°S
South Shetland Islands
South Orkney Islands
Deception Island
Antarctic Peninsula
Rothera
WEDDELL SEA
0
500
km (approx)

TILTING THE GLOBE

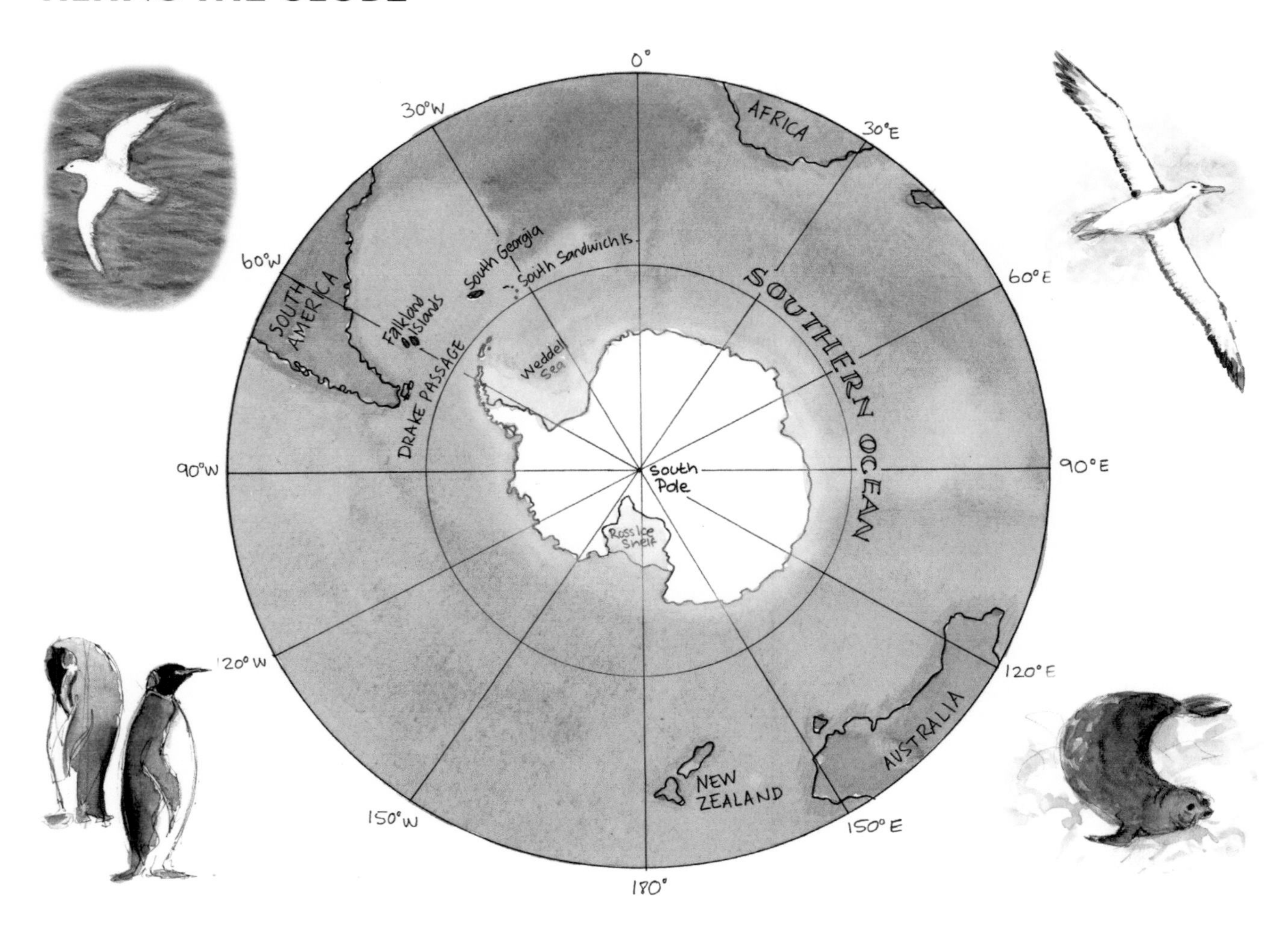

The continent at the bottom of the world is almost out of sight on a conventional globe. On a Mercator projection schoolroom map it becomes stretched beyond all reason, a meaningless ribbon of white at the bottom of a page in which all the important stuff, the bits we need to learn about, are everywhere else. When I found out in November 2020 that I was going to Antarctica, I bought an old National Geographic map of the continent on eBay and pinned it on my wall. Everything depends on your point of view; now I was looking at the world from underneath, from the axis of its spin – if you stand at the south pole, is there a still small place where the earth isn't spinning at all?

I often wondered, as a child, why the world map was drawn with north pole at the top and south pole at the bottom. Was there a big sign in space, pointing at the earth, saying 'This way up?' Maps are drawn by the explorers who lived to tell the tale, and nearly all of them were from the Northern Hemisphere. The words 'top' and 'bottom' have many layers of meaning and I wonder how different world history and politics would have been if the globe was turned upside down. Try it when you get the chance – it makes the familiar suddenly very unfamiliar indeed.

The continent of Antarctica was a feature of many maps for centuries before its existence was finally proved. Known simply as *Terra Australis Incognita* (unknown southern land), it seems to have been the early Greek mathematicians who first suggested that there ought to be a southern land mass to balance the amount of land in the Northern Hemisphere. In spite of the Church's insistence for a while in the Middle Ages that the earth was flat, the idea of a Southern Continent endured and became the ultimate goal for maritime explorers who were quite used to the spherical nature of the world and, with a combination of courage, luck and navigational skill, were getting on rather well exploring it.

Cook came close to the elusive *Terra Incognita* on his second voyage from 1772-75.

'I now reckoned we were in the Latitude 60 degrees south and farther I did not intend to go, unless I met with some certain signs of soon meetings with land. I was now tired of these high Southern Latitudes where nothing was to be found but ice and thick fogs'.

Cook's sailing master on board *Resolution* was Joseph Gilbert, a skilled navigator and chart maker. This is my copy of Gilbert's chart from Cook's voyage south. Nothing to see here!

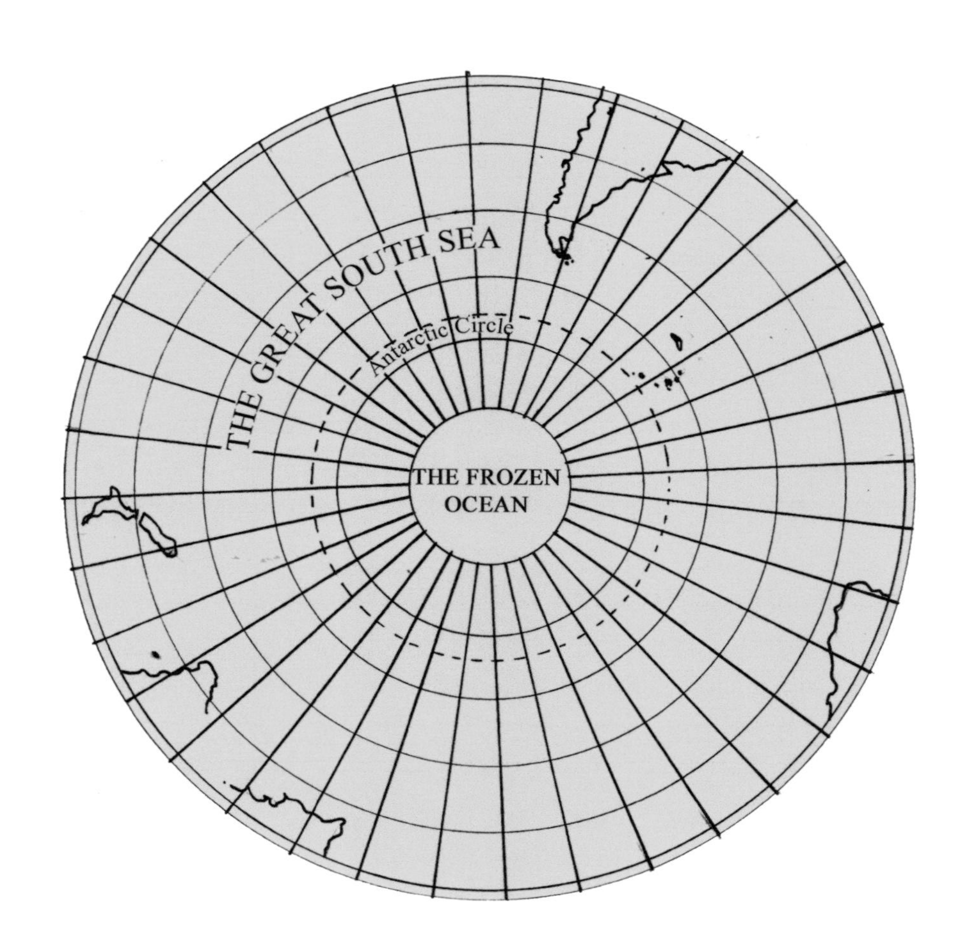

In spite of coming within 120km of the Antarctic Peninsula, the 'ice and thick fogs' meant that he turned back without ever knowing how close he had been. At the end of his voyage he concluded:

'The risk one runs in exploring a coast in these unknown and icy seas, is so very great, that I can be bold to say, that no man will ever venture farther than I have done and that the lands which may lie to South will never be explored'.

My National Geographic map of Antarctica was printed in 1957 when I was a year old and the world was still very much a resource; global warming and conservation were far from mainstream ideas. The notes on the map give some revealing insights into the mindset of the time:

'Coal deposits prove that Antarctica once supported vegetation. They are low-grade lignite, impractical to mine. Almost certainly oil will be found under the ice'

'Whales and seals abound in Antarctic waters. The fur seal, however, is practically extinct, only the seals without soft underfur survived man's slaughter. Most of the world's whaling is carried on here, it constitutes Antarctica's only industry.'

Fortunately, change was already in the air. 1957 was International Geophysical Year in which 12 countries committed to undertaking scientific research in Antarctica. This laid the foundations for the International Antarctic Treaty which was signed on 1st December 1959 in USA. In summary, the Treaty:

- sets aside disputes over territorial sovereignty
- prohibits military activities such as the establishment of military bases or weapons testing and prohibits nuclear explosions and the disposal of radioactive waste
- guarantees freedom of scientific research and promotes international scientific co-operation with scientific results exchanged and made freely available
- provides for the inspection of all stations, ships and equipment in Antarctica to ensure compliance with the Treaty
- covers the area south of 60′ latitude

In more recent times, environmental protection, not considered a high priority at the time that the Treaty was signed, has come to the top of the agenda and the Treaty has been substantially added to over the years. There are now 53 member nations. This means that Antarctica is now protected by some of the most stringent bio-security and environmental measures on the planet, which is just as well given the rapid increase in high latitude tourism over the last ten years or so.

It is extraordinary how much has changed in my own lifetime. In these planet-conscious times, Antarctica is now very much centre stage. In just over a century it has changed from a place described by travel writer Sara Wheeler as 'a testing ground for men with frozen beards to see how dead they could get' to a tourist destination; from a land-grabbing potential resource to the most protected environment on the planet. It's where scientists monitor the health of the planet. Images of retreating glaciers and breaking icebergs encourage our desire to recycle more and consume less, even when we may only have a vague idea how the two things are connected. Documentaries and photos of scientists of all nations working together to help save the world with their ice cores and weather balloons have added to our enduring fascination with this extreme continent of ice, penguins and explorers – the world's biggest desert and perhaps our last great wilderness.

So how come I was lucky enough to go there with my sketchbooks?

Artist in Residence

There is a rather splendid building in Cambridge called the Scott Polar Research Institute. It was founded in 1920 as a memorial to Captain Scott and his companions who died on the South Pole expedition in 1912 and soon developed into a centre for polar research as well as a place where polar travellers could meet, study and add to the extensive archive and museum.

'SPRI's mission is to enhance the understanding of the polar regions through scholarly research and publication, educating new generations of polar researchers, caring for and making accessible its collections (including its library, archival, photographic and object collections), and projecting the history and environmental significance of the polar regions to the wider community for public benefit.'

I managed a quick visit to the Polar Museum before leaving for Antarctica – this is the outfit worn by Frank Debenham, one of the survivors of the Scott expedition who was instrumental in founding SPRI.

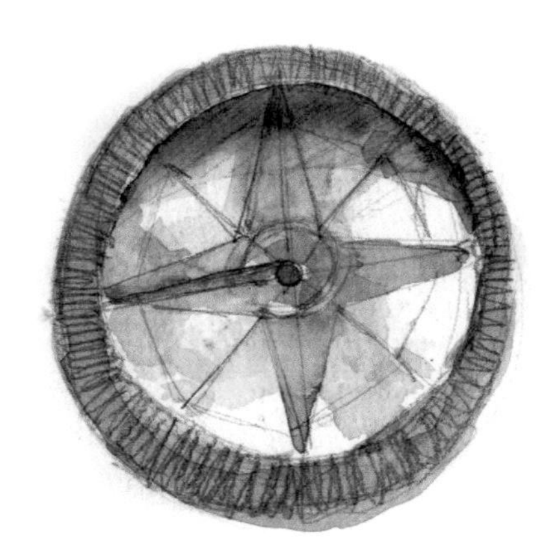

A few years ago I'd met artist Shelly Perkins who had been to Antarctica as Artist in Residence for the Friends of Scott Polar Research Institute and showed me some of her sketches and artwork. It didn't occur to me then to find out more until November 2020 when Shelly tipped me off that applications were now open for the next year's Antarctic Residency. I decided to put in a bid.

I got it – so much to my surprise that the organisers had trouble contacting me. I saw a number I didn't recognise on my mobile but didn't think to check who had been phoning.

A year later the trip finally took place. The residency takes place on board the Royal Navy's ice patrol ship HMS *Protector*, which was in dry dock undergoing maintenance at the time of my appointment. I had to wait until the next austral summer to join her in the Falklands for one of her month long work packages in Antarctic waters.

Quarantine

In those covid-troubled years, travel was complicated and a ship is no place for a serious virus. Neither is an isolated island group with limited medical facilities, so the Falkland Islands Government insisted on strict quarantine for incomers. This is how I came to be one of only a few civilians at RAF Linton-on-Ouse in Yorkshire, a disused air base run by the Army as the Forces quarantine unit for troops on overseas postings.

It was one of the strangest eight days of my life and I have only one sketchbook page to show for it, but it was a time of catching up on emails, making the best of it and reminding myself of the very good reasons why I was there. We were housed in groups of six called cohorts, each kept separate to avoid cross contamination and regularly tested for covid. If any one in the group tested positive, the group would have to start the quarantine period again.

The practice of quarantine is centuries old but the name comes from the Venetian rule of making a ship wait 40 days at anchor before being allowed ashore (the word comes from the Italian 'quarantina' meaning 40). That must have been hard on crews who had sailed far and would be desperate for the pleasures of shore, within sight but out of reach. The choice of 40 days could have been for medical reasons or it could have been Biblical. In ancient times the popular phrase '40 days and 40 nights' was just another way of saying 'a long time', but it has connotations of being a time of cleansing, renewal or rebirth. I was truly thankful that my quarantine was only 9 days and not 40.

How different sea borders are from land borders. The legacy of ship quarantine still makes itself known. When I first started sailing back in the 1980s we learned to fly the quarantine signal flag 'Q' on first entry to a foreign port. This flag means 'I require free pratique' – or in today's terms: 'We have just arrived and are disease free, may we come ashore?'

Doodling the blues... experimenting with my palette

For the first couple of days in my Yorkshire quarantine my brain was a blank and I found it hard to feel remotely creative or interested in anything except hiding under a duvet escaping into the novels I'd brought to read on the plane. I was too lethargic even to tackle all those routine admin tasks lurking in my laptop, including over 70 unanswered emails and messages. But once I had sorted out my wifi, borrowed an electric heater, begged some teabags, bought a bottle of wine via our group leader who was able to place orders with the local shop, I began to feel better placed to make the most of this unexpected gift of time. Our routine included strict timings for meals (12.16 for lunch...) so that we were separated at all times from the other cohorts. My companions, all service personnel, were in their twenties or early thirties. They treated me with courtesy, keeping me informed of any changes to our routine.

They knocked on the door when it was mealtime so that we could all walk across to the canteen together and that was the chance for brief conversations about their hopes and dreams of travel, promotion, family, in the 20 minutes allocated to eat and clear our table. In the evenings they chatted outside their rooms with a few cans of beer and snippets of conversation drifted by – '...nobody over the age of 35 has sex, do they?' Wisely, I did not join in!

Apart from mealtimes and walks around the camp, I spent most of the time in my room, playing around with my watercolours whilst watching Youtube clips from British Antarctic Survey, following all kinds of threads on google, and catching up with friends too. 'Goodness!' said one, 'You actually answered your phone!' My bottle of wine, chilling ineffectively on the window ledge was enjoyed with friends each evening via video chat or zoom, using my phone as my source of wifi (the base wifi was very limited). After a carb-heavy lunch I was happy to miss supper.

Essential supplies arrived by post – a towel, which I'd forgotten to pack, more teabags, peanuts and the cold weather gear I ordered before I left but which didn't arrive in time. Warm jacket, lined mittens and snow boots!

For daily exercise I took a walk on the disused airfield and amongst the once-busy grey concrete buildings.

There was a tense day close to the end of the quarantine period when we received a message that there was covid on the camp and we might all have to start quarantine again, but at the last minute, when the tests for our group were clear, we boarded the coach for the flight from Brize Norton to Mount Pleasant and the journey properly began.

FALKLANDS

HMS *Protector* is the Royal Navy's only icebreaker and her task is to patrol the waters of the Arctic and Antarctic, making herself useful in ways that I gradually came to understand a little more as the voyage progressed. From November to March each year she is based in the Falklands, spending five weeks at a time in Antarctic waters before coming back to refuel and provision.

I joined the ship on 25th November, was welcomed on board and shown round, delighted to find that my cabin belonged to an officer on leave and was rather spacious, with its own bathroom. As the only civilian on board, I was an outsider in a very closely knit world though treated with courtesy by everyone I met.

Having already met the ship's chaplain on the flight, I was pleased to find that his cabin was next door to mine. The chaplain is usually a good ally on an unfamiliar ship as they have more free time than everyone else and are inclined by their calling to be helpful to strangers! Michael (nicknamed 'Bish' by the crew) proved to be good company and very knowledgeable about birds.

FALKLAND ISLANDS
FRIDAY
26th November Bertha's beach, Falklands. 4 mile walk from

Friday 26th November: *Revd Michael has the cabin next to mine and asks if I want to accompany him to see the gentoo penguins at Bertha's Beach, about four miles away. I'm pleased to discover that there is somewhere to go to within reach – the ship is berthed at Mare Harbour which is close to the base at Mount Pleasant but a long way from anything else. It's about 1500 before we head off down a long track but it's good to be out walking again in such wide open spaces under a clear blue sky. There's a cool breeze blowing, but Michael is in shorts and tee shirt.*

Once we reach the beach I stop to sketch and he goes into the water to look for Commerson's dolphins. He has with him an empty drinks can full of stones as he has heard that rattling the can under the waves will attract the dolphins. It does, and although I can't see them from my perch up the beach I can hear his whoops of delight as he tries to photograph them playing in the waves around him.

nmerson's dolphins play in the surf; Revd Michael has waded into
sea & rattled a tin of stones to attract their attention. It obviously works!
all shells actual size ...
arch of gentoo penguins with Revd Michael. So good to be back on these islands!

A mile or so further on we find the gentoos. They are quite shy penguins so I sit by the dunes so that I can sketch at a distance. There's no time for more than a few quick scribbles with the brush pen but it's exhilarating to be here and to have made a start on my sketchbook. It's late afternoon by the time we set off to walk the five miles back to the ship but the sun is still high. Back on board just after 1900, too late for supper but time for a welcome g&t and a handful of peanuts from my stash. (I left most behind in Linton, but managed to bring one packet!)

Gentoo penguins on the shore
watched by a mean-looking skua
Gentoo penguins, Bertha's Beach
white sand, big shells!

giant southern petrel
white-rumped sandpiper
South Atlantic tern
2-banded plover
HMS Protector, Mare Harbour, Falklands
Sunday 28th November

Sunday 28th November: *A day punctuated by various safety drills. My challenge is to work out which ones to ignore, which ones to respond to and where to go for each one (the hold for enemy fire, port side of main deck for lifeboat if we're sinking, and conference room or wardroom for anything else). Later in the day there's a tour of the emergency gear on board and we get to climb inside one of the two claustrophobic lifeboats hanging in davits on the upper deck.*

Monday 29th November: *There was the chance of a lift to Stanley early this morning with the Captain and Commander who had a meeting with the Governor. I set the alarm and was ready by the gangplank for 0730. They dropped me off in the main street and I had three hours to spare. Everything was still shut but it was a sunny day and I found a spot out of the wind by the cathedral to make a study of the whalebone arch with* Protector *in the background, picked out in stones on the far hillside along with all the other ships who patrol these waters. I went to the visitor centre to buy wifi but to no avail; none of the wifi hotspots were even vaguely lukewarm so I had to give up. The gift shop opened at 11; I had a mini shopping spree and then it was time to meet the car. Back to the ship in time for a late lunch.*

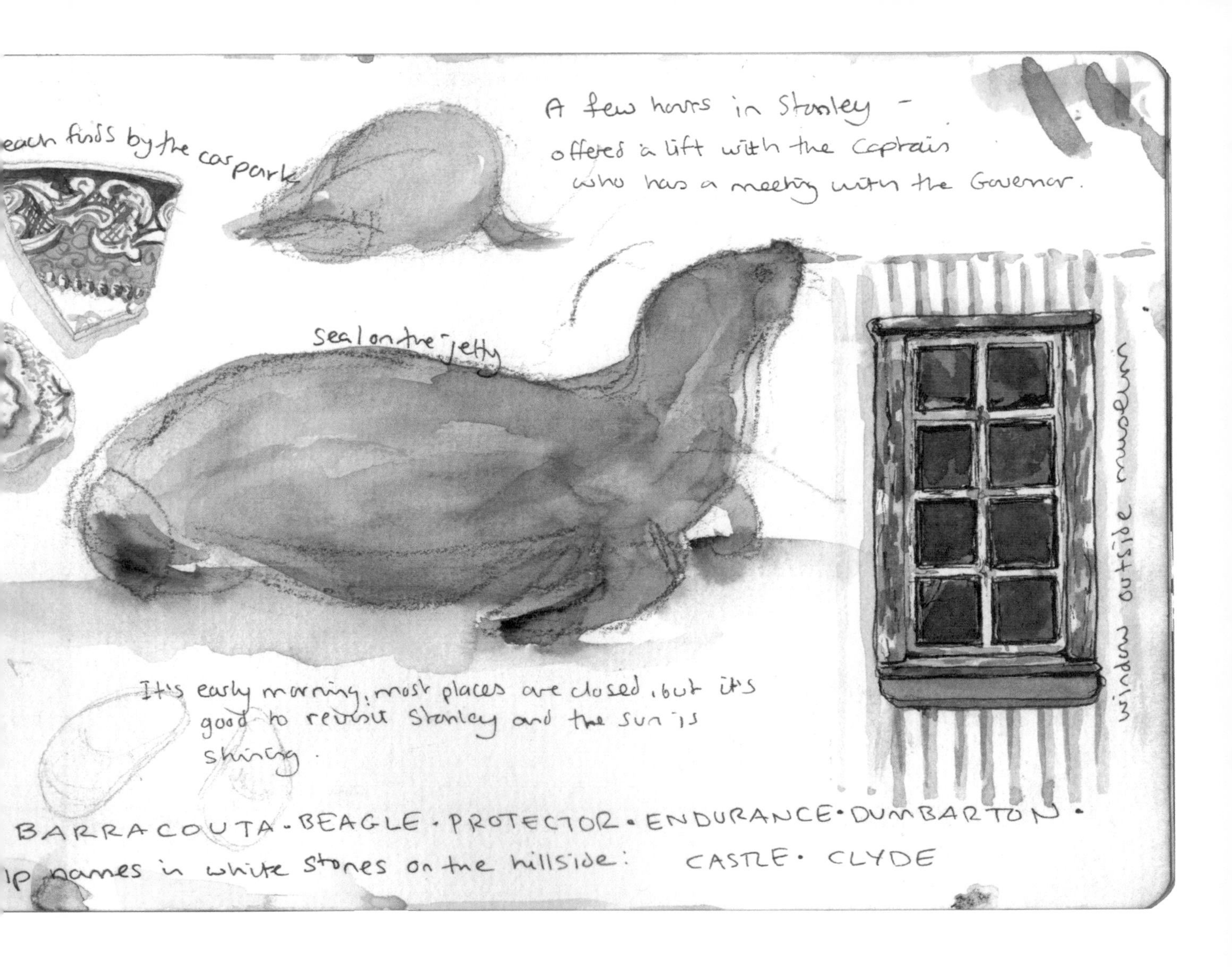

each finds by the car park
A few hours in Stanley -
offered a lift with the Captain
who has a meeting with the Governor.
seal on the jetty
window outside museum
It's early morning, most places are closed, but it's
good to revisit Stanley and the sun is
shining.
BARRACOUTA · BEAGLE · PROTECTOR · ENDURANCE · DUMBARTON ·
names in white stones on the hillside: CASTLE · CLYDE

I had last visited the Falkland Islands two years before, sailing into Port Stanley on board the Dutch ketch *Tecla*, thrilled by the sight and smell of land after a four week non stop passage from Easter Island. That adventure, recorded in my book *Sketchbook Sailor*, inspired my desire to return to this wild Southern Ocean. I spent ten days in Port Stanley before flying home, getting to know this quirky place and friendly people. Vivid memories remain of long off-road landrover trips to see the penguins at Volunteer Point and enjoy a picnic among shipwrecks and whalebones at Whale Point; being given a lift by landmine removers when caught in a storm; spending long hours in the museum immersed in the fascinating history of the islands.

Dropped anchor Port Stanley 11.48.
First impressions....
very cold & windy. All the
winds we didn't get in the
last few days are
blowing now

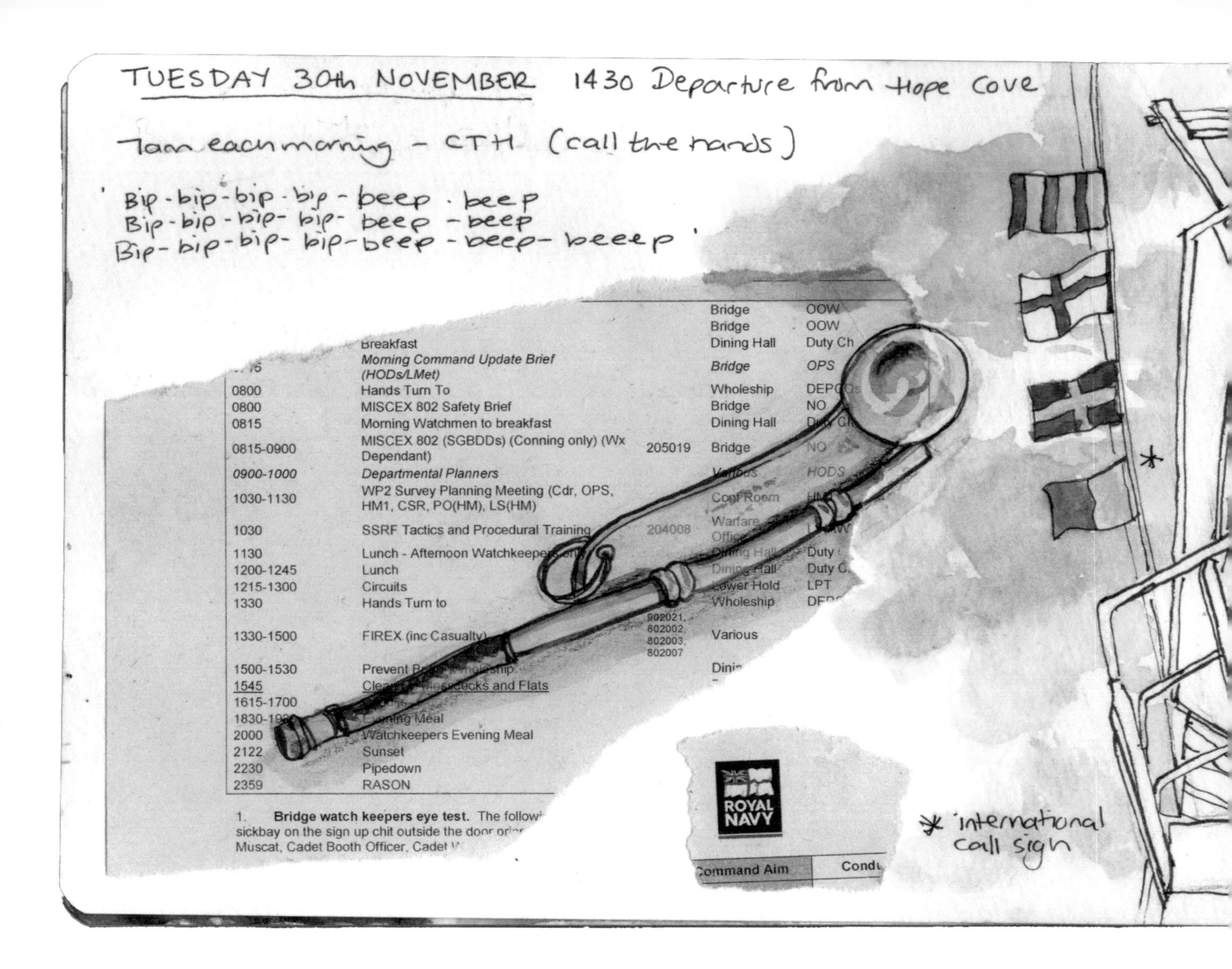

TUESDAY 30th NOVEMBER 1430 Departure from Hope Cove
7am each morning - CTH (call the hands)
'Bip-bip-bip-bip-beep-beep
Bip-bip-bip-bip-beep-beep
Bip-bip-bip-bip-beep-beep-beeep'
Bridge OOW
Bridge OOW
Breakfast Dining Hall Duty Ch
Morning Command Update Brief (HODs/LMet) Bridge OPS
0800 Hands Turn To Wholeship
0800 MISCEX 802 Safety Brief Bridge NO
0815 Morning Watchmen to breakfast Dining Hall
0815-0900 MISCEX 802 (SGBDDs) (Conning only) (Wx Dependant) 205019 Bridge NO
0900-1000 Departmental Planners HODS
1030-1130 WP2 Survey Planning Meeting (Cdr, OPS, HM1, CSR, PO(HM), LS(HM)
1030 SSRF Tactics and Procedural Training 204008
1130 Lunch - Afternoon Watchkeepers
1200-1245 Lunch Duty C
1215-1300 Circuits LPT
1330 Hands Turn to Wholeship
1330-1500 FIREX (inc Casualty) 902021, 802002, 802003, 802007 Various
1500-1530
1545
1615-1700
1830-19
2000 Watchkeepers Evening Meal
2122 Sunset
2230 Pipedown
2359 RASON
1. Bridge watch keepers eye test.
Muscat, Cadet Booth Officer, Cadet
ROYAL NAVY
Command Aim
* international call sign

Tuesday 30th November: *On our way! We finally leave the dock just after 1100, then the ship spends a couple of hours manoeuvring around the harbour testing her gear, tugs in attendance. I'm pleased to meet Belinda, ship's photographer, hopefully she will be after similar viewpoints to me when we get ashore. When we finally head to the open sea I'm prepared for rough seas – I've taken the ginger and seasickness tablets and when the sleepiness kicks in I head for my bunk.*

Waking up later, I'm surprised to find that the motion is gentle. On deck, it's a sunny afternoon with a gentle sea running, a cool breeze but not yet cold.

Going into the wardroom for a cup of tea, the assembled officers tell me that I'm invited to the Captain's cabin for a drink. One of them offers to take me up there – I'm horribly aware that I look crumpled, wearing my tracksuit bottoms and no time to freshen up, but too late. Captain Michael Wood welcomes me and pours a rum cocktail for us. Courteous and handsome, he's been Captain of HMS Protector *for two years, lives on Dartmoor with his family.*

He reassures me that if there's anything I need I'm to ask, and he'll make sure that I get as much opportunity as possible to go ashore. If anything, his kindness makes me feel slightly fraudulent, as if I really do need to produce some artistic masterpieces to make up for the attention I'm getting!

After my large rum and coke I head to my bunk. The gentle motion sends me into a long deep sleep full of dreams.

Wednesday 1st December: *The good weather continues. After my long sleep I'm grateful to discover I don't feel at all seasick, and head out on deck with my bag of sketching gear. I've always found that when the motion of the sea isn't making me ill, it makes me very well indeed – as if this is where I belong. There's a clear blue sky, a cool wind and a sapphire blue sea flecked with whitecaps. Astern, a flock of prions swoop above the wake. Also called 'whalebirds' they are small and graceful with a 'V' shaped marking across the wings. Above the prions, an albatross hovers and tilts. Michael ('Bish') comes over with his bird ID app and tries to work out whether the prions are Antarctic or Fairy – we think Antarctic.*

Tuesday 30th November -- leaving harbour
Thursday 2nd December. Slight sea, easy motion & a grey day..
View from the Bridge

r sunny day, force 4, slight swell. It doesn't take long for birds to follow in our wake -
white underwing black edge
fast moving
force on downward tilted wing tips
shape of wing tips
December - Wandering Albatross, Antarctic Prions + Southern Giant Petrel
day 3rd December. Views from the stern (starboard side). overcast, light wind,
ger swell from the west.

Thursday 2nd December: *I thought it was about time I plucked up courage to go to the Bridge. You're supposed to say 'Officer of the Watch, Bridge Please!' as you go up the final stairs, but not being sure who to address the request to I just gabbled it at the person nearest, a young cadet of 19. There was only the Captain up there along with trainee officer Miriam and one or two others. 'He's the youngest on the ship', said the Captain, nodding towards the cadet. 'Well, I'm certainly the oldest!' I replied. I should sketch the Bridge in action, perhaps later when it's a bit more 'in action'. So far I've shied away from sketching any of the crew, except for a quick line drawing of the Captain and his number one giving the order to cast off lines.*

Supper when under way is 1830; Rev Michael has told me where to find the day's Orders, the list of events for the next day, but in this world of acronyms, I can make little sense of most of it. There are things I need to know about tomorrow – another LFT (lateral flow test for covid) in preparation for South Georgia, handing in my passport for a South Georgia stamp, and a lecture for all on preparing for cold weather.

Friday 3rd December: *This afternoon we had a lecture on cold weather gear by the leader of the marines, spiced with expletives '.... if it doesn't fit properly, it will be f..... useless when it's f...... freezing out there. Any questions? No? Happy days. Right, who can remember the five ways that the body loses heat?' (Convection, conduction, radiation, evaporation, respiration – worth remembering!)*

There was also a demo on how to layer up your standard issue Forces cold weather gear, (wolf whistles attended the entrance of a young marine dressed only in thermal underwear). I'd been invited by young stores officer Kasey to pay her a visit if I needed anything. She gave me boots, socks and a waterproof over-jacket in case my oilskin jacket wouldn't fit over my down jacket, but everything else I reckoned I already had.

The marines' presentation was followed by a shorter talk from ship's doctor Alex, who without any expletives at all warned us of the dangers of frostbite, snow blindness and hypothermia. (All easy to catch, easy to prevent, hard to treat if not caught early.)

SOUTH GEORGIA

Saturday 4th December: *I'd set my alarm for 0530 as we were told there would be a good chance of seeing the solar eclipse if the skies were clear. I slept fitfully, pulled on slippers and jacket when the alarm went off and went out on deck. There was no sign of the eclipse, which apparently had come and gone a bit earlier, but the sight that faced me in the early morning sunlight was far more thrilling – a mountainous coastline, jagged peaks tipped with snow and the white wedge of a glacier. South Georgia! I sketched fast as we steamed gently past, and caught some of the excitement of the moment. Within half an hour the island had disappeared into the fog so I took the chance to go back to bed for a couple of hours.*

South Georgia has always been on my island wish-list. It's a remote, inhospitable heap of mountains and ice on the edge of the Southern Ocean. There are no towns, roads or airport, yet there is a fabulous museum, with a UK postcode – SIQQ 1ZZ – and it's been a British Overseas Territory since 1775 when Captain Cook landed and named it Georgia after King George III. He and his officers found it far less inspiring than I did, naming the southernmost headland 'Cape Disappointment':

'I did flatter myself from the distant soundings and the high hills about it, we had got hold of the Southern Continent, but alas these pleasing dreams are reduc'd to a small Isle, and that a very poor one too'

(from the log of Cook's Second Lieutenant Charles Clerke)

cerulean

5.30 am Saturday 4th December 2021 First impressions of South Georgi
By 6 am the mist had increased & the island disappeared.

indigo

FORTUNA GLACIER on the north coast of the island as we steamed eastwards to King Edward Cove

cad. red

raw sienna

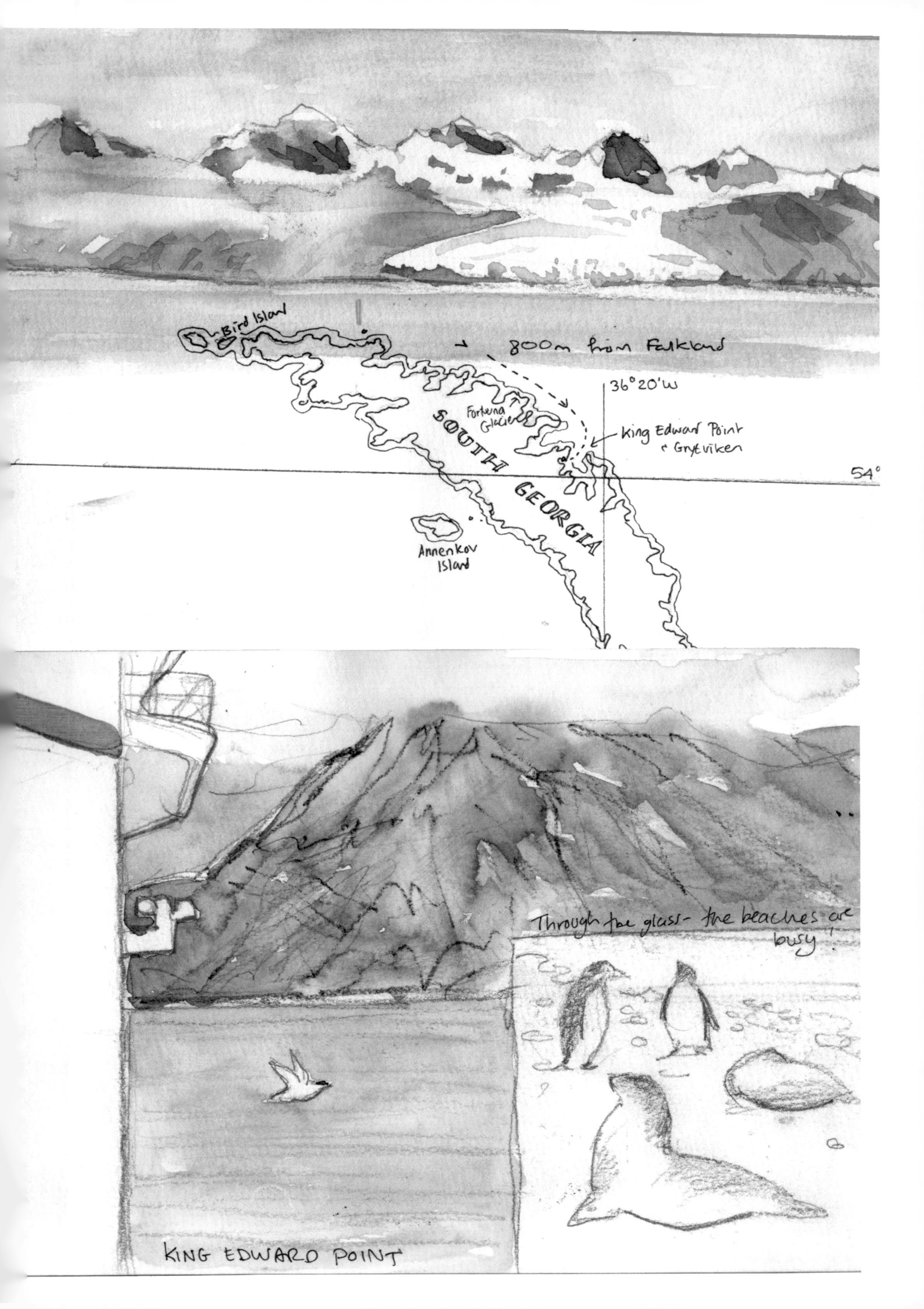
Bird Island
800m from Falkland
36°20'W
Fortuna Glacier
SOUTH GEORGIA
King Edward Point
& Grytviken
54°
Annenkov
Island
Through the glass - the beaches are busy!
KING EDWARD POINT

SOUTH GEORGIA WHALING MUSEUM
GRYTVIKEN
Approaching Grytviken. James Cair
goes on ahead to check depths by
quayside.
where snow meets sky, where ice meets sea
Monday 6th December
NORDENSKJOLD GLACIER
Greene Peninsula

und is the next bay, Maiviken. the ship holds her position with DPS
(Dynamic Positioning System) whilst RIBs are launched & a team go
ashore with building materials for the S.Georgia team.
hard hats on main deck
Ship's crane can lift up to 60 tons
crane
ing harbour
Monday 6th December
2pm
Leaving King Edward Point.
Rocky Pt.
Right whale Rocks
MAIVIKEN
CUMBERLAND EAST BAY
GRYTVIKEN
KING EDWARD POINT
King Edward Cove
Greene Peninsula
NORDENSKJOLD GLACIER

Saturday 4th December 2021
SOUTH GEORGIA WHALIN
EUM
GRYTVIKEN
KING EDWARD POINT
RESEARCH STATION
'VIOLA' (left)
'ALBATROS' (right)

Now a thriving conservation area, South Georgia is home to thousands of fur seals, king penguins and albatross, who are able to breed there safely thanks to strict safeguarding and the elimination of rats. But the island has a human past that's a mix of dark and heroic. Most people know of Shackleton's incredible open boat voyage in 1916 from Elephant Island and his trek across South Georgia's glaciers and mountains to fetch help for his stranded crew, but in the 19th and early 20th century, South Georgia was a focus for sealing and whaling on a major scale. Cook's discovery of the island opened the way for seal hunters who were forced to search ever southwards as numbers of both fur seals and elephant seals (killed for their blubber) dwindled in easier waters. By 1820 fur seals on South Georgia were almost extinct and by 1825 the sealing era was over.

To walk on South Georgia's shores now where the noise and smell of seals fills the bay is a humbling experience and a reminder that with enough will and good management the tide can be turned.

By the 1890s whalers had begun to head south for the same reason as the sealers – whales had been hunted to extinction in northern waters and ships were forced to search ever further from home. South Georgia became the base for seven whaling stations. At Grytviken alone, 175,000 whales were processed between 1905 and 1965 when it became unprofitable. There were simply no whales left to catch.

Saturday 4th December: *I came on deck to find us in a bay, the ship holding station whilst the survey boat went inshore to check if there was enough depth of water to come alongside. There was. I went up onto the bridge deck to watch us motor further into the bay, to a small jetty at King Edward Point. After lunch, the South Georgia government representative, Vicki Foster, came on board and gave a welcome talk including where we could go, how crucial biosecurity is and how to deal with aggressive seals.*

I went ashore as soon as I could after hoovering out my pockets and rucksack to eliminate risk of unknowingly taking foreign objects and seeds ashore. I'd seen photos of South Georgia, the rusty ships and old whale processing plant, the dramatic mountains and wildlife, but nothing prepared me for the real thing. The clarity of the light, the stony beaches alive with families of fur seals, basking in the sunlight, grunting and braying; skuas and great southern petrels hovering nearby hoping for a supper of baby seal; Antarctic terns calling and skimming on the shoreline and small groups of placid king penguins. Above all the smell! The tang of fresh grass and flowers, clear mountain air and the acrid, almost sweet smell of seal poo. The natural world in full force amongst the ruins of human gear for exploiting it. Whalebones litter the shoreline, seals bask on the old slipways and decaying jetties.

Outside the museum at the old whaling station of Grytviken in the warm sun I sketched two decaying whaling boats, the Viola *and the* Albatros, *streaked with rust.* Viola *was built in Hull as a fishing boat and there is talk of trying to bring her back to UK and restore her. The* Albatros *was built in Norway. I had a quick look at the museum and chatted to curator Jayne, made a plan to come back for a proper look on Monday so that I could make the most of the sunshine for outdoor sketching.*

Terns wheel overhead and seals doze in the sun amongst the ruins of the old whaling station. More rust stained wrecks and old wooden boats lie beached on the shore, against a backdrop of snow capped mountains. So much to sketch – I need at least a week here! Back to the boat late afternoon, dodging seals dozing or growling warily along the track. Happily tired and realising that this day was very special – up there at the top of the list alongside Cape Horn, Panama Canal, Galapagos.

Then it was time to have a shower and change into something reasonably smart as I'd been invited to dine with the Captain and guests. We met for drinks first in the Wardroom, and I soon realised there was no need to feel nervous or awkward as the guests turned out to be lovely Vicki, the Governor, and her young assistant Josh. From the ship there was also first officer Tom, ship's doctor Alex, Ops manager Rory and another officer David. Conversation was fascinating from all sides – life at sea, life on the island, the work that's done down here towards conservation and the challenges that come with that. Dinner was served in the conference room, the port was passed to the left, and then we all went back to the wardroom where the other officers joined us, the drinks flowed and the evening became more informal, full of long intense conversations forgotten the next day. A good time had by all.

In our conservation-aware times, whaling is abhorrent and you might think that the ruins at Grytviken would be gloomy and oppressive. There is a melancholy there, of course, but a strong feeling that the present is now more vibrant than the past. I found it useful to put whaling in context. It belonged to a time before we dug our oil from the ground and whales were, simply, large and very useful fish.

Life at a whaling station was incredibly bleak, with long absences from home, isolation and little comfort. There is a church at Grytviken, recently restored. It was consecrated on Christmas day 1913 by a clergyman who noted that his congregation were 'young men in the prime of life, all weather-beaten and hardy, clearly bearing the marks of their toil. Christian life unfortunately does not wax strong amongst the whalers'.

'Below 40 degrees south, no law; below 50 degrees, no God.'
(whalers' saying)

THE LAST WHALERMAN (inspired by a day at Grytviken)

I was just a young man when first I went to sea
We shipped on board *Viola*, my brother Tom and me
The sea was full of whales and we were full of need
To fill our holds with blubber and our families to feed
Don't be too hard on whalers, don't damn us for our deeds
We were simple sailing men, fishing for our needs

We caught them and we hauled them, dying to the shore
We pulled them up the slipway to strip them to the core
The work was long and hard and the wind blew icy cold
As we filled our tanks with blubber and our pockets full of gold
You can say we wasted nothing, you couldn't ask for more
As we stripped them and we boiled them on that cold South Georgia shore

We're homeward bound for one last time, I'm weary in my mind
Our ship's hold now lies empty, there were no more whales to find
Now sixty years have passed and the whalers life is lost
You've learned the sea has limits and everything its cost
Don't be too hard on whalers, for our slaughter on the sea
For I was just a sailor and they were just fish to me

Viola she lies rusting on that cold Grytviken shore
I am in my grave and the whaling is no more
The blubber tanks are empty, crumbling into rust
Has history taught us something? I surely hope it must
Don't be too hard on whalers, for our slaughter on the sea
For I was just a sailor and they were just fish to me
Don't be too hard on whalers but stop to question why
You haven't learn the lesson not to fish the ocean dry

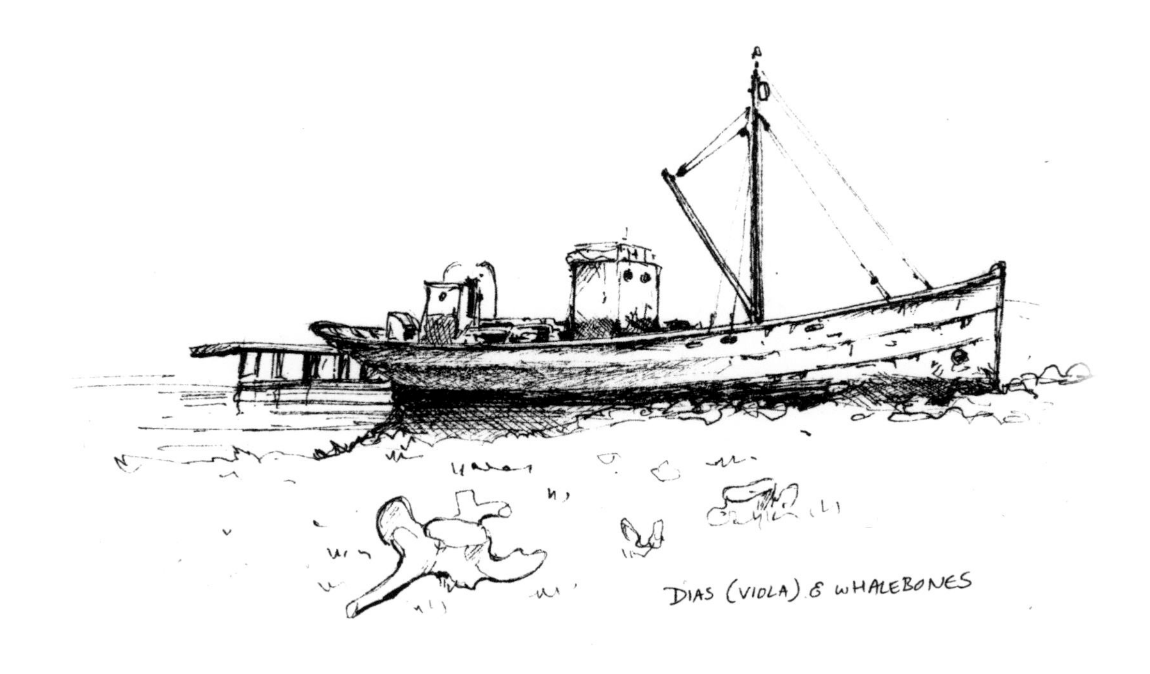

DIAS (VIOLA) & WHALEBONES

Looking east from Grytviken
WHALE BONES ... litter the shore

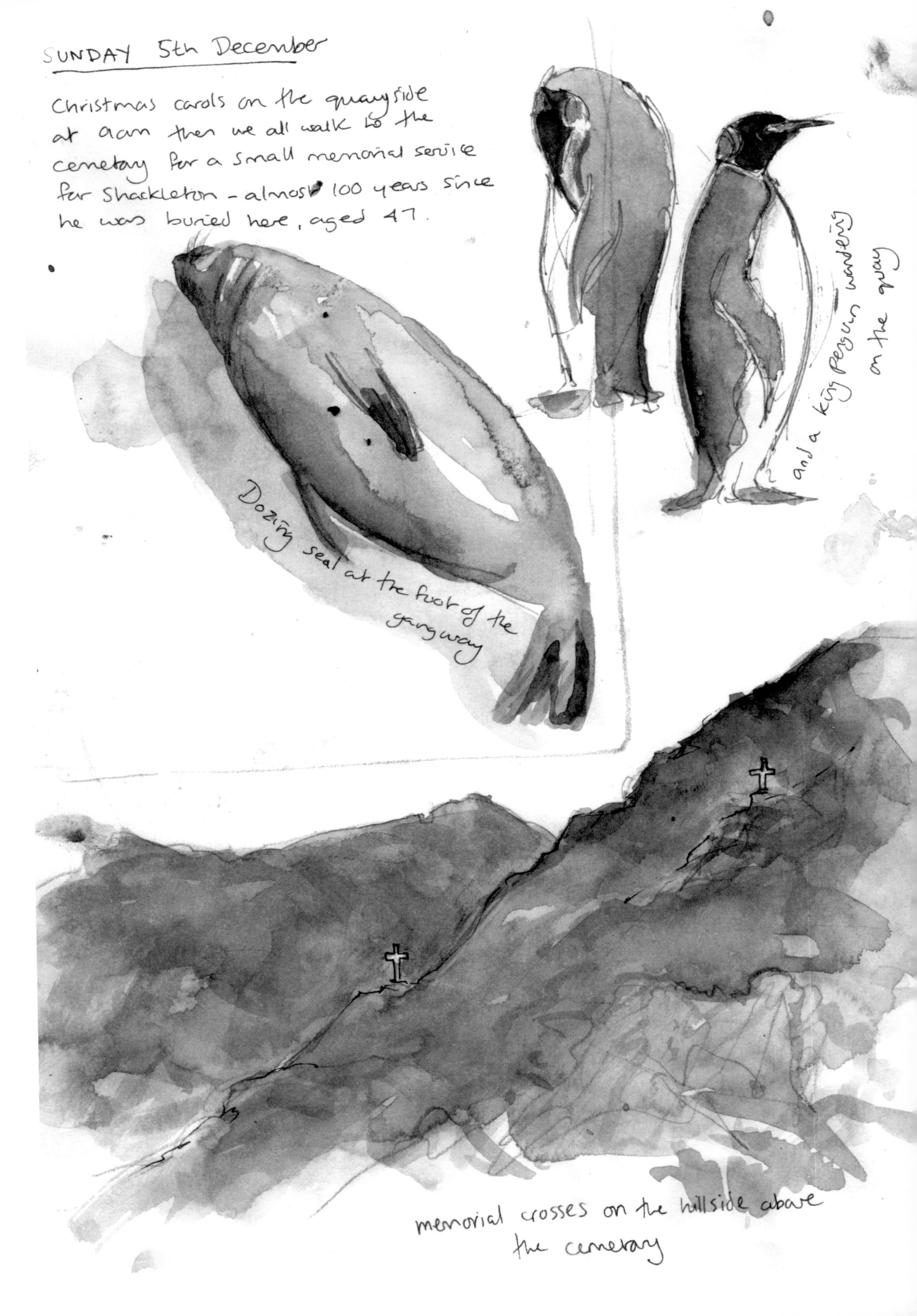
SUNDAY 5th December
Christmas carols on the quayside at 9am then we all walk to the cemetary for a small memorial service for Shackleton – almost 100 years since he was buried here, aged 47.
Dozing seal at the foot of the gangway
and a Kig penguin wandering on the quay
memorial crosses on the hillside above the cemetary

'stand at ease'
hands behind back,
feet shoulder-
width apart
correct hand position
for 'stand at ease'
demonstrated by
Miriam - left hand
under right hand
At Shackleton's grave on
South Georgia with
HMS Protector
Still an inspiration
100 years on for
the new generation
of Antarctic Explorers
- HMS Protector
5 Dec 2021
In remembrance
HMS PROTECTOR
A173

SUNDAY 5th December

walk up to Shackleton memorial on St. Edward's Point in the afternoon. Very windy! On the run from a very bad-tempered seal on the way back who was lying in the track

KING PENGUINS on the beach at King Edward Point.

Snarly seal blocking the path . . . "
.. King penguin taking no notice of humans at all .

Graveyards, whaling and conversation with a sculptor

'I have often marvelled at the thin line which separates success from failure'

(Ernest Shackleton)

On 5th January 1922 Ernest Shackleton died of a heart attack on board his ship *Quest*, which was anchored in the bay at Grytviken. He was 47. He had returned to South Georgia with a new expedition intending to explore the lesser known islands of the Southern Ocean and more of the Antarctic continent.

His body was initially taken by a whaling ship to Montevideo to be returned home to his family, but a telegraph from Emily Shackleton requested that her husband be buried on South Georgia, close to the wild places that he loved. His headstone is the largest in the small whaling cemetery on Grytviken shore.

Sunday 5th December: *Today the ship's company held a memorial service for Ernest Shackleton at his graveside. We are just a few weeks short of the 100th anniversary of his death.*

It took time to get everyone lined up in rows, standing at ease and looking smart in their cream jumpers and blue berets, whilst Belinda set up her camera gear and a drone was launched to take overhead footage. I stayed outside the cemetery, sketching the scene from the hillside.

After the service, I'd planned to do some sketching at Grytviken – more rusty hulks beckoned, and the atmospheric whaling station. But I met Michael Vissochi, a Scottish sculptor who is spending time on the island gathering inspiration for an installation about whaling; specifically, the flensing plant. This was the area where whales were dragged up onto the shore for skinning and stripping the carcass. It was a grisly business and there is only empty space now and the remains of a slipway where this took place. Michael's task is to create something in the space that will put it into context and give visitors some insight into its significance.

We went to the museum to chat out of the cold wind and had a cup of tea in the kitchen at the back, along with Jayne the curator. Michael wanted to record our conversation as we chatted happily over tea and ginger nuts about creativity, sketching, pens and pencils, imagination and empathy.

Here's a link if you'd like to find out more about Michael's work on South Georgia: sght.org/commission-grytviken-whaling-station-south-georgia

SOUTH SANDWICH ISLANDS

The South Sandwich Islands rise steep-sided out of the sea, glaciers and shrieking wind spilling down the face of the dark mountains. Like South Georgia, the islands are a British territory, but nobody lives in this land of wind, rock and ice. It's home to penguins, snow petrels and other birds who thrive on the rich southern seas and seem to care little for the cold. When you look up at those uncompromising peaks and glaciers, the idea that anyone can own such wild places as these in the first place seems somewhat absurd.

Cook was unimpressed when he first sighted the islands in 1775, which he named after the Earl of Sandwich.

'It would have been rashness in me to have risked all which had been done in the Voyage, in finding out and exploaring a Coast which when done would have answered no end whatever, or been of the least use either to Navigation or Geography or indeed any other Science'

Nearly 250 years later, there are still areas of the sea around these islands that have not been mapped in detail. One of HMS *Protector*'s tasks was to fill in some of the gaps and help to bring the charts up to date.

A day of surveying meant cruising up and down across a defined area while sensors on the hull sent data back to the computers on the bridge. Hydrographers (known as 'droggies') then analysed this information to make a detailed map of the depths of the sea bed. What a difference three centuries have made to seafaring! I watched the hydrographer sitting in shirtsleeves on the bridge focussing on a computer screen of dots and numbers whilst in my mind I imagined an 18th century sailor feeling his way through uncharted waters on a cold deck with nothing but a piece of lead on the end of a rope to let him know the water's depth.

The only discomfort we suffered during surveying was alternating periods of calm and rough conditions; calm when the ship cruised with wind and waves behind her, then suddenly rougher as she turned to track a parallel course the other way, against the elements. In the galley, non-slip mats stopped our meals sliding off the table but walking to the table with a plate of food required some care.

Wednesday 8th December: *Tomorrow's orders tell us that we'll be arriving at Saunders Island around 0800 and there will be two shore parties – I'm on the list for one of them! I will have to don a survival suit and climb down a long rope ladder to the RIB. The reason we're calling at at Saunders Island is that the ship has been asked to assess the size of the chinstrap penguin colony here – no, we don't have to count them individually, the drone will be used to take photos of the penguins from above.*

First iceberg spotted today – a big slab of white on the horizon.

"down upon the Southern Ocean sailing,
down bellow Cape Horn

Thursday 9th December: *Saunders Island is a volcano streaked with snow. The narrow shoreline is brown scree dotted with penguins and fringed with surf and sea ice. The wind is raw. By 0930 the ship is holding her position with DPS and along with the rest of the shore party I'm dressed in a rather fetching orange survival suit with helmet and lifejacket. A bit like an adult babygro. It's hard to walk around as the built-in boots are big and heavy, but it's certainly keeping the wind out.*

We watch the first RIB party skirt the shoreline for a safe place to land, and it takes them time. I must confess not to be too disappointed when the news comes back on the radio that there will be no second trip, conditions are just too tricky. Off comes the survival suit and it's back in my own clothes for a bracing sketch or two up on the bridge deck before spending most of the rest of the day in the warmth of my cabin, adding more detail to my drawings.

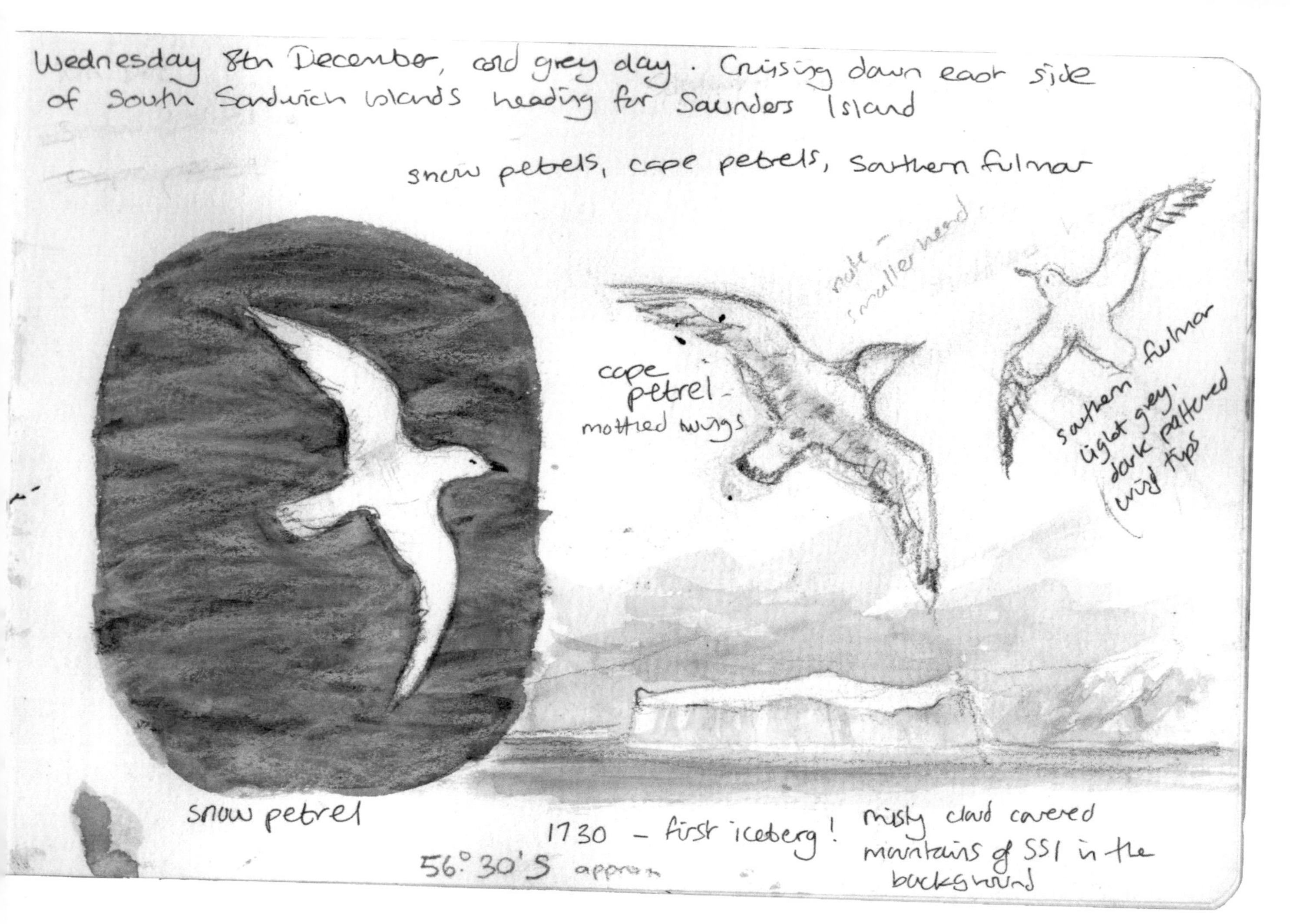
Wednesday 8th December, cold grey day. Cruising down east side of South Sandwich Islands heading for Saunders Island
snow petrels, cape petrels, southern fulmar
cape petrel - mottled wings
southern fulmar light grey, dark patterned wing tips
snow petrel
1730 - first iceberg!
56°30'S approx
misty cloud covered mountains of SSI in the background

Friday 10th December: *It was a bouncy night, hard to sleep when being thrown around in my bunk. Looking out of the Wardroom window while making my morning tea I could see that we were rolling beam on to a swell in murky weather with mountains and a few icebergs looming out of the fog. The land ahead is Thule Island and further, hidden by the mist, is Cook Island. We are here to do some surveying but until swell and visibility improve, we can't get into the caldera – the remains of the volcanic crater – between Cook and Thule Island. So we are cruising up and down the southern shore, surveying the uncharted waters there. The deck is out of bounds and the only outdoor space accessible is the undercover vaping area on the deck close to my cabin. There's not much of a view from there but I can still sketch the sea.*

I've got to know two young crew, Phoebe and Kasey, who call into my cabin when off duty for a sketchbook update. They were delighted that I had drawn both of them! Phoebe loves to draw, using her tablet to produce very effective digital art.

Later, I went on deck one more time. We were close to land now, the texture and coldness of glacier and rock feeling close in the wind. A single snow petrel skimmed the wavetops and the grey skies glowed silver white above the ice.

Saturday 11th December: *Early this morning the ship navigated her way into the centre of the caldera. To the west, the curved rim of the volcano is Thule Island and to the east, the smaller Cook Island forms the other edge of the crater. Icebergs and scattered rocks lie at the open ends. The water was more sheltered here, just a low swell running, whilst shrieking gusts blew the surface of the water to spume. I put on every layer I had and found a fairly wind-free place up on the Bridge deck to sketch the island and glaciers.*

I was told to be ready for a trip ashore in the RIB at 1330. There were 18 of us pulling on survival suits, helmets and lifejackets. This time there was no last minute cancellation – I was going down that long rope ladder to where the inflatable zodiac, looking very small, surged in the swell below. The crew offered to tie a safety strop around me to help me down, but I have my pride and managed unaided. It was hard to feel each rung of the ladders wearing the heavy survival suit with its built-in boots. Slowly, slowly, concentrate, down to the last rung and wait for the command – now! – as the gap between boat and ship closed momentarily and I stepped on board.

We were soon wet with spray, but thanks to the suits the only part of us getting cold was our faces. I was thrilled to be out on the water so close to the glaciers. We were making for a shelving beach full of penguins at the end of the island, but there was too much swell and it was too rocky to risk landing. We then headed across to the other end of the island, near the ruin of the old Argentine camp buildings, but the problem was the same there, so we went back to the ship and it was rope ladder time again.

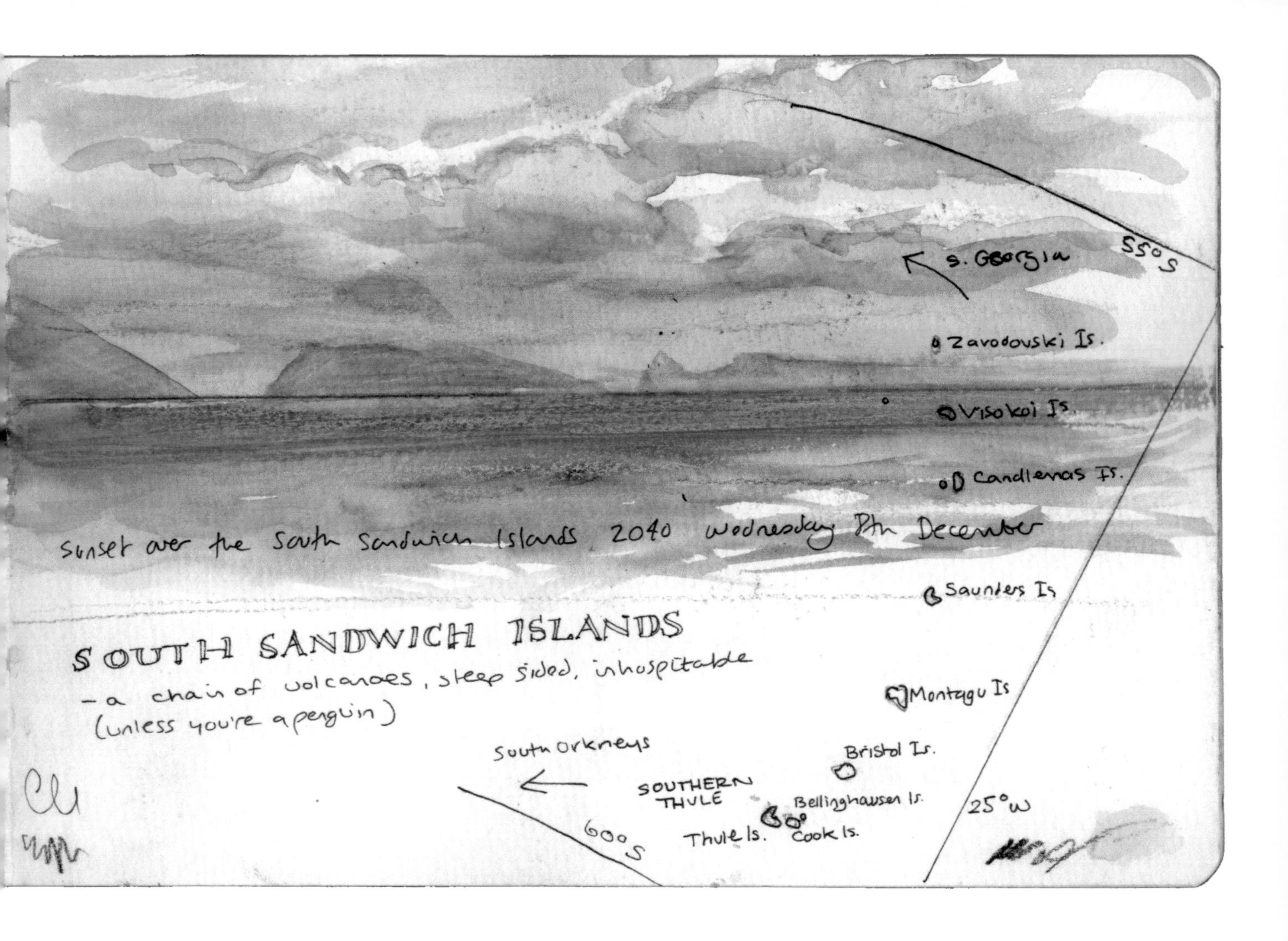

The tricky bit is the step from boat to ladder as there is only a second to grab the ropes and get a foot on the rung before the gap becomes too wide. I managed fine and took it slowly up the ladder, getting the thumbs up from the crew.

Beyond the known world

Captain Cook was expressing his feelings about this icy wilderness when he named this island Southern Thule. In ancient Greece and Rome, Thule was an island so far north it was almost off the map. 'Ultima Thule' (farthest Thule) came to mean anywhere that was beyond the known world. Having been named and claimed by Cook, it's now governed – if governed is the right word for such a place – by the UK as part of 'South Georgia and South Sandwich Islands' (SGSSI). On our abortive search of a landing place, we came close to a lonely ledge of rock where wreckage of twisted steel and concrete stood out on the skyline, the remains of an Argentinian naval base established in 1972 in attempt to assert Argentina's claim to the islands. It was removed by the British after the Falklands war in 1982. What did the men stationed here think of the political decisions made far away that led them to spend lonely and pointless months on this bleak ledge of rock? The idea that anyone at all can possess such a wild place seems vain and absurd.

For HMS *Protector*, her surveying complete, it was time to head south again.

Thursday 9th December. Approaching Saunders Island
first thing this morning. I was invited to go ashore in the RIB with
the second shore party but there was too much surf & conditions
getting worse so the 2nd trip was cancelled. At least I got to put on
my survival suit, lifejacket & helmet!
TODAY I AM MOSTLY WEARING ....
*
merino top & leggings
skinny jumper
wool guernsey jumper
sailing jacket
lined walking trousers
sailing boots
down body warmer
hat & snood
thick woolly socks
* with a few layers in reserve
couple of 'buffs'
gloves & mittens
Friday 10th December
cad. red + cerulean (sea-grey)
cad. red + ultramarine (sky-grey)
cape petrel
How do we define 'beauty'?
THULE ISLAND
Douglas Strait
Hanging around off
Thule Island .... survey work
waiting for the morning
going into the
caldera
Force 6 & rolling!

aunders Island, South Sandwich Islands - volcanos, snow capped.
Home to chinstrap penguins, and the ship is here to count them ... (luckily
ey have a drone to get an approximate idea of size of colony!)
ector' holds her position in the bay using DPS* (too deep to anchor)
Icebergs - big ones
e Island
View from the Bridge
looking aft. Thule
Island. Cook Island, fog
ice + rock.
Extreme
wilderness
+
extreme
technology

Saturday 11th December.
Approaching the entrance to the caldera at Southern Thule.
View from the deck
COOK ISLAND
Sunday 12th December
Survey work on east of caldera (close to Cook Island) in the morning.

from the Bridge
calmer waters inside the caldera but with fierce gusts. Survey boat launched.
LAND of SEA, ICE & ROCK
am taking bearings on bergs & rocks
end of Cook Island, patterns & rhythms of rock & ice ...
... snow petrels dance in the wind

Sunday Service in the Conference Room …
Amy accompanying hymns on flute

" … **Preserve us from the dangers of t
sea and of the air** … "

memories of childhood … the sea voyage home 1969

Hymn – Eternal Father

Eternal Father, strong to save,
whose arm hath bound the restless wave;
who bidd'st the mighty ocean deep,
its own appointed limits keep.
O, hear us when we cry to thee,
for those in peril on the sea.

O Trinity of love and power!
Our brethren shield in danger's hour;
from rock and tempest, fire and foe,
protect them wheresoe'er they go.
Thus evermore shall rise to thee,
glad hymns of praise from land and sea.

views of Thule Island south side whilst sur

Monday 13th December

1343 GMT - entered Antarctic waters (60° south)

very lumpy sea -
managed my laundry, be
change, a sea sketch
not much else!

HMS PROTECTOR 30th November —

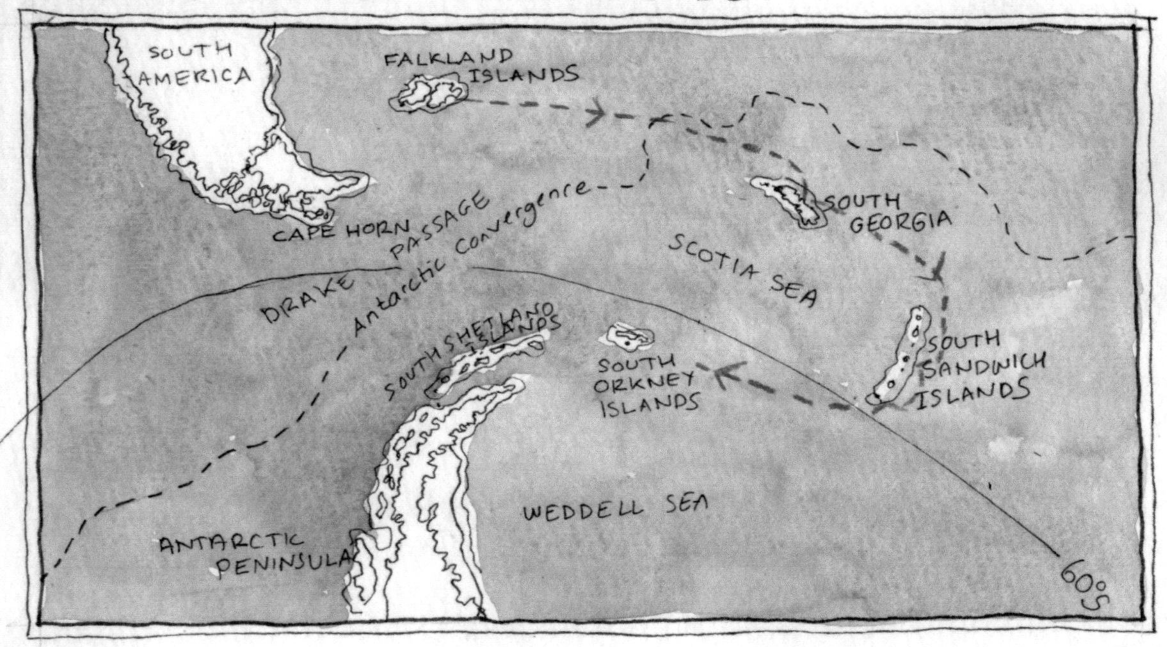

-day 14th December

Tuesday 14th Decembe
pm - sunshine
a cloud of
Cape petrels, Antarctic prions, snow petrels
ys, 1900 14th December
Approaching Coronation Island.
South Orkneys
Coronation Island

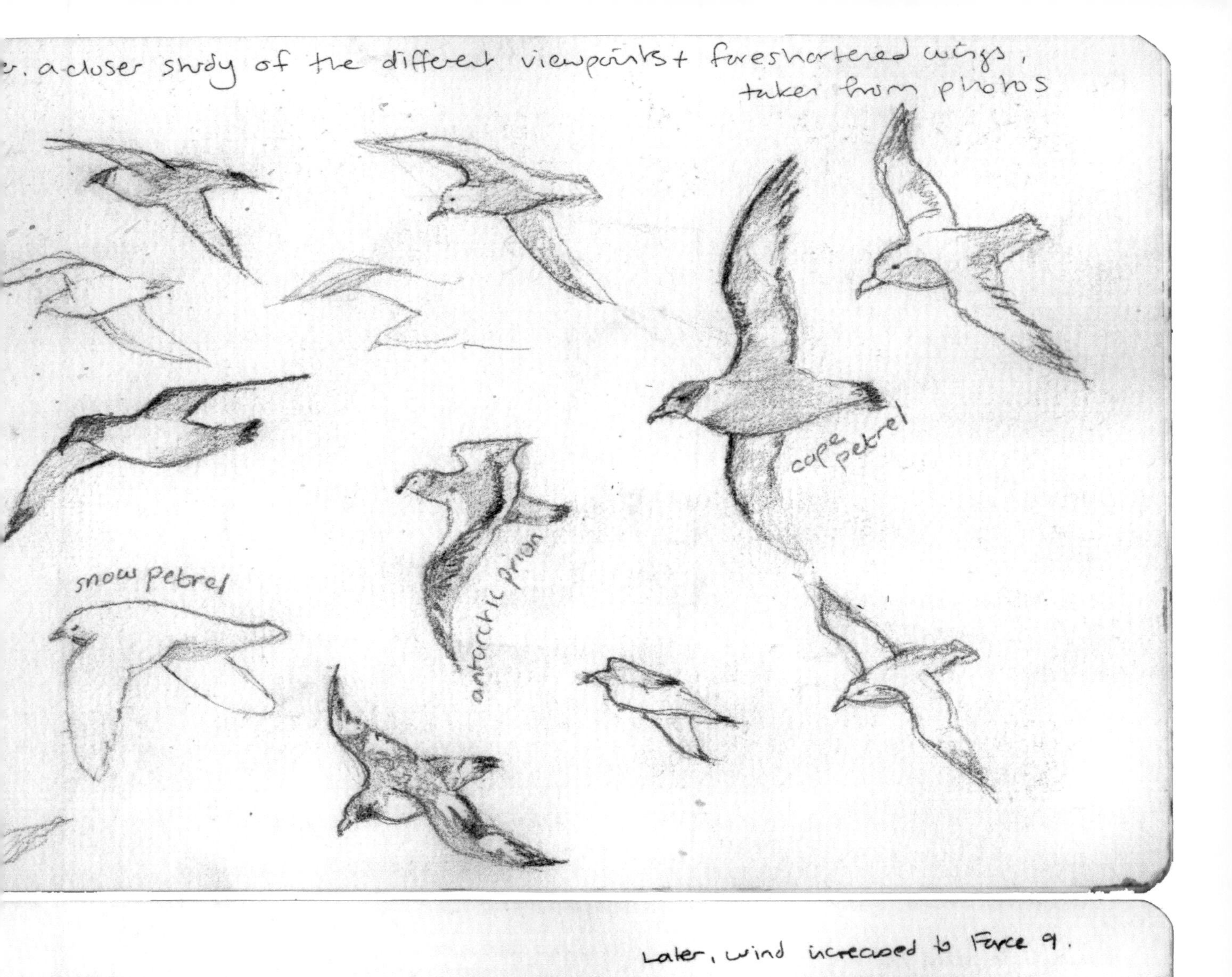

a closer study of the different viewpoints + foreshortened wings, taken from photos
cape petrel
antarctic prion
snow petrel

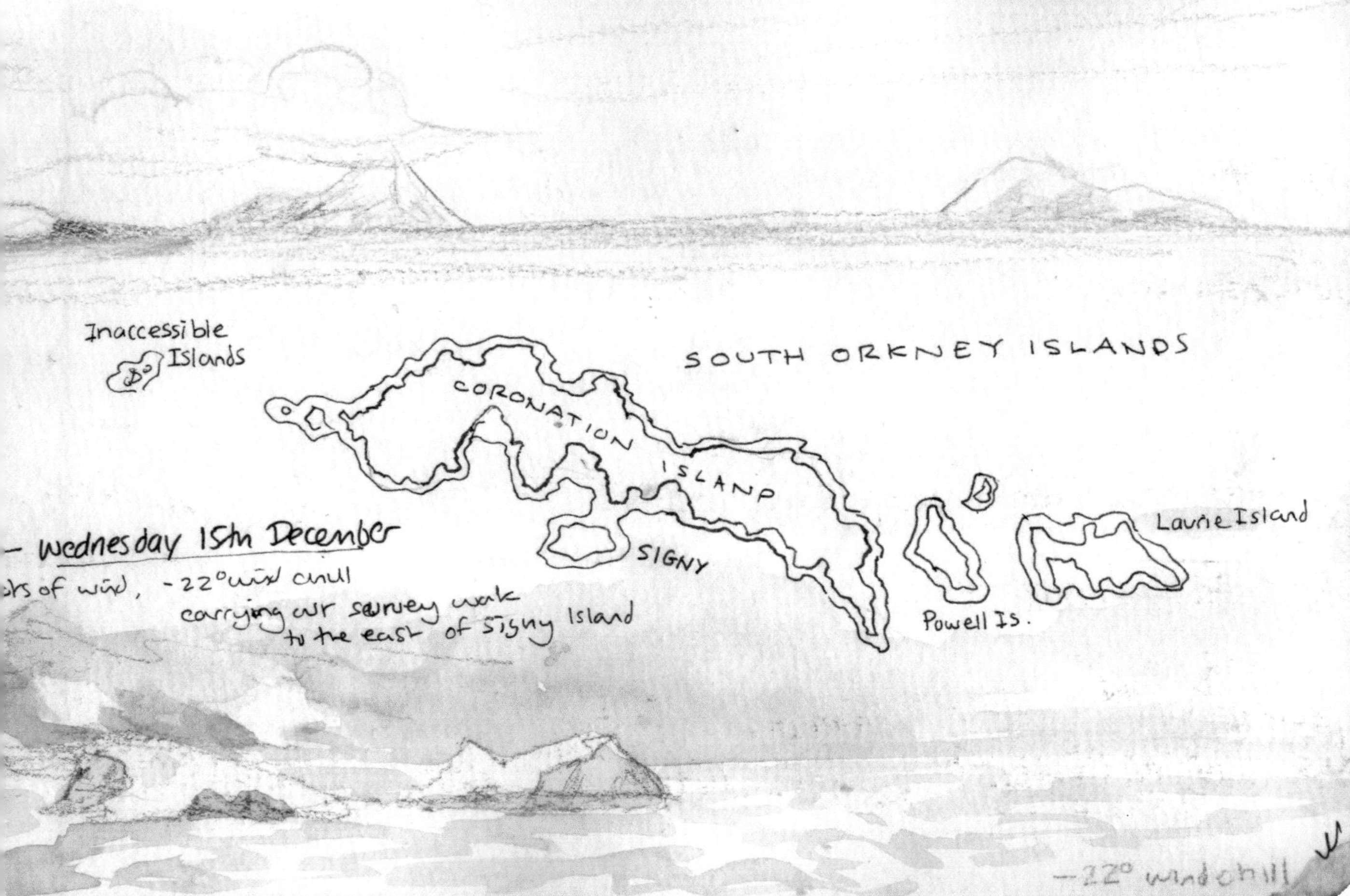

Later, wind increased to Force 9.
Inaccessible Islands
SOUTH ORKNEY ISLANDS
CORONATION ISLAND
SIGNY
Powell Is.
Laurie Island
– Wednesday 15th December
of wind, -22° wind chill
carrying out survey work to the east of Signy Island
-22° windchill

15th December
Rocks, wind & iceberg
Zooming in close on an iceberg - a few black dots are penguins
The glacier's edge....
16th December, survey work close to Coronation Island
later: trip ashore on Signy

the ship taking soundings as close to the glacier as she can get
edge of the ice sheet at the edge of the retreating glacier...
17th December 8pm

SOUTH ORKNEYS

Monday 13th December: *A sea day, quite rough, ship is pitching. Feeling a bit muzzy headed but managed to do my laundry and change bedlinen, do a sea sketch. Didn't fancy lunch and reckoned missing a meal or two would be a good idea anyway. Fell asleep in the afternoon.*

Plenty of time to read and think. There is a small ship's library – a cupboard outside the wardroom – with a good variety of books. I'm currently reading Joanne Harris' The Strawberry Thief... *a little strange, but interesting on the theme of change: 'life is on loan, and all the things we find on the way – lovers, children, happiness – have to be given back in the end'*

At 1343GMT we crossed the 60th parallel, which puts us now in Antarctic waters.

The Antarctic Treaty of 1959 defines Antarctica as everywhere lying south of 60 degrees latitude. When our ship crossed this invisible border, an announcement was made on the Bridge.

The South Orkneys, which lie just south of 60 degrees, were discovered by two seal hunters in 1821, an American and a Brit who gave the islands their original name – Powell's Group. Two years later James Weddell renamed them South Orkney Islands as they are on roughly the same latitude south as the other Orkney Islands are north.

Our destination was the British Antarctic Survey base on the island of Signy, where there was some inshore surveying to do, and the promise of a trip ashore.

Wednesday 15th December: *A grey murky day, blowing hard but we're surveying on the leeward side of Signy Island, south of Coronation Island, so the sea state stayed reasonable all day even when the wind went up to force 9. Wind chill was minus 22 degrees centigrade. The weather is supposed to improve tomorrow so the plan is for some trips ashore.*

Thursday 16th December: *I was down for 'First Stick' ashore today (why is a shore party called a stick? I don't know) but the time was yet to be announced. I went up to the Bridge early as the ship was getting closer and closer to a glacier, surveying for the first time a bay that had previously been covered in ice. A startling and very real result of global warming. Part of the ship's task here is to survey the bay used by the BAS base, as well as the wider brief of mapping the sea bed where data is scarce for the Hydrographic Office.*

After lunch I rummaged around for a small survival suit, could only find medium so had to make do with that. Luckily our run ashore was in the hard bottomed RIB which meant no climbing the long rope ladder. Instead, we boarded into the boat in its davits and then it was lowered into the water. We landed at a jetty by the BAS station, currently unmanned and with several dozen very large elephant seals dozing around the cluster of steel huts. The captain had taken ashore a sack of Christmas goodies for the base scientists who'd be arriving on the island from the RRS Sir David Attenborough *before Christmas, so photos were taken holding the sack in front of the door – the captain, me in a pixie hat and medic Alex in a Father Christmas hat!*

There were a few penguins – gentoo, chinstrap and Adélie further along the shore. The elephant seals ignored us so I walked along the shoreline and did a rapid sketch of the base with mossy hillside behind – no grass here. My hands didn't get too cold but I worked quickly, then did a bit of penguin sketching and a pencil sketch back on the pier, planning to finish everything off back in my cabin.

This evening the sky cleared and the lowering sun turned the snowy hills of Coronation Island to pink and gold. We are not yet far enough south for perpetual daylight, but late evening is a soft twilight. I went on deck when I saw a couple of icebergs through my window, but then someone said 'Look the other side!' and there, close to, glittering mother of pearl in the sunlight, was the biggest block of ice I had ever seen. It was more than an iceberg, it was the very essence of cold. I photographed it, videoed it, and sketched it, drawing only the outline and indications of shadows with blue pencil on the spot, racing to get as much down as I could before my hands became too cold. In a few seconds I'd got what I needed and back in the cabin threw paint at the shapes until I was happy that I'd captured that feeling as best I could.

Everyone was in a bit of a holiday mood after that. It was 2200 when we were watching the iceberg but we were putting the clocks back an hour tonight, which means extra sleep. Michael offered to buy me a drink and join the off duty crew in the wardroom. I gladly accepted.

Sunday 19th December: *Very boisterous sea state. A bit of drawing this morning, a sea sketch, then I discovered there was a yoga session at 1215 so I went to that – run by the fitness instructor 'Basher'. I've been keeping away from all things gym related but enjoyed this gentle stretching session on mats. There was too much motion for any exercises standing up. Then at 1330 it was church service – goodness, such a lot of structure in a sea day! Rev Michael does conjuring tricks to illustrate his sermons and says he doesn't mind at all having a heathen along to join in the singing.*

'The presence of "cold"

20th December. Lizzie on watch.

Friday 17th December, 10pm

gentoo
imperial shag
Gentoo - long orange beak, pink feet
Chinstraps - flattish heads
Adelie penguins - small v. poin beak orange/bl colouring
Chinstrap penguins
v. dark heads, wider blunter beaks than Adelies
gentoo face - an - very strange!

B.A.S. Station,
Signy, South Orkneys
60°43'S 45°36'W
Thursday 16th December

Thursday 16th December

British Antarctic Survey Station on Signy.
South Orkneys (currently unmanned)

Gentoo, chinstrap & Adelie penguins on the shore. Colony of Elephant seals snoozing round the buildings.

SIGNY ISLAND

16th December 202

no grass; colours of moss on the hillside and lichen on the rocks

BRITISH ANTARCTIC TERRITORY

POST OFFICE

The sign on the door:

SIGNY ISLAND RESEARCH STATION

Signy Island, South Orkney Islands
60°43'S. 45° 36' W

Signy Island is an active United Kingdom research station which is occupied during the summer by staff of the British Antarctic Survey.

Please do not enter the site except in a emergency. Please do not tamper with any equipment or installations both at the station or elsewhere on the islan The safety of British Antarctic Surve staff and the outcome of their scien and monitoring programmes depend upon all the equipment remaining fully serviceable.

If you enter the station complex you do so at your own risk and on the understanding that neither the British Antarctic Survey nor the Government of the British Antarctic Territory will be liable for any personal injur or damage to property that you ma sustain.

Please leave the station safely closed when you depart and inform the British Antarctic Survey of your visit.

(sign also in Spanish and Russian)

Signy Station
weathervane on hut by slipway
JOHN BISCOE
STANLEY FI
old harpoon heads outside the BAS hut
On the beach -
stones and
whalebones
(no wood, no plastic)

ANTARCTICA

Monday 20th December: *Antarctica is in sight! A lumpy morning bashing into waves – the view from the Bridge was spectacular, a shower of spray as the bow rose and fell. Later, the Officer of the Watch announced that the Peninsula was off the port bow. A hazy spine of mountains, topped with cloud and snow, scattered icebergs lined up on the horizon in front of it.*

I have loved our slow approach to this longed-for place and the island-strewn curve that our voyage has taken. You can get to the Antarctic Peninsula from the mainland in three days, but we had been three weeks at sea, noticing the gradual increase of icebergs, wildness of the landscape and abundant bird life.

When people think of Antarctica, they think of the continent itself – that mysterious white mass at the bottom of the globe, explored by stubborn heroes and inhabited by scientists. But my journey with HMS *Protector* took me to maritime Antarctica, to the long peninsula that stretches out towards South America and forces the Southern Ocean to squeeze through the 1000 mile gap known as Drake Passage. With the icy tip of Antarctica at one side of this gap and Cape Horn at the other, this stretch of stormy water has inspired fear and fascination in sailors for centuries.

Our voyage followed in the wake of sealers, whalers and maritime explorers who charted the ocean around the continent and came to know the islands that lie like stepping stones between *Terra Incognita* and the known world.

Where does the sea end and the land begin? Antarctica is an ambiguous place where the division between land is sea is blurred by islands and ice. It wasn't until the British Graham Land Expedition of 1935 that the Antarctic Peninsula was finally known to be part of the continent and not a series of islands. Fringed by islands and ice shelves, it would be hard to tell, especially at the northern, narrowest part of the Peninsula, known as Graham Land.

1635 20th December - Antarctic Peninsula on port bow
3 weeks after leaving Falklands

The dramatic mountainous scenery here is very different to the vast plateau of the Antarctic continent and when the contours of land are blurred by ice sheets, who can tell which is land and which is sea? The British Graham Land Expedition itself was undertaken in a small and under-funded sailing ship *Penola* but had the valuable assistance of aerial reconnaissance in a De Havilland Fox-Moth aircraft. A bird's eye view of the landscape made life a lot easier for the map-makers than trying to make sense of a maze of ice and rock.

Most place names in Antarctica reflect the expedition leaders, captains, kings and admirals back home. Graham Land, the northern part of the peninsula, was named by English explorer and whaler John Biscoe in the 1830s after Admiral Sir James Graham. Very few are named after ordinary sailors, men who lived with the knowledge that each day might be their last; where the navigator had a sextant but no charts, where the only safety lay in the sharp eyes of the lookout by day and a combination of prayers and good luck at night or in fog. For us, an iceberg is a thrilling sight, a moment of wonder of beauty. For early sailors, it must have been terrifying.

'the frost and cold [were] so intense as to cover the Rigging with Ice, like compleat christal ropes, from one End of her to the other, and even to stiffen our outer Coats on our backs, yet Capt. Cook would not allow any fire in the Gally, or anywhere else but at proper times in the day.'

(from the log of one of Cook's officers)

What would those early pioneering sailors have thought of the comforts of HMS *Protector*, or one of the many small cruise ships that visit these waters? Even in rough weather, I reflect that I have never felt so safe in my life. Everything is taken care of and I know I am going to get home again.

Tuesday 21st December: *We're in Antarctica proper now, a day of clear skies and warm sunshine in Gerlache Strait with Anvers and Brabant Island on one side and the Antarctic Peninsula on the other. We're surrounded on all sides by high mountains shaped by snow and ice that looked close enough to touch but are in fact at least 15 miles away.*

Up on the bridge deck this morning with Belinda and Michael we saw a couple of humpbacked whales breaching and blowing, but they didn't find us interesting enough to get too close. I sketched mountains, ice and sky. I stood on deck looking, breathing air that felt like drinking champagne. The day's circuit training took place on deck rather than in the gym. I didn't join in!

Clarity of light is so intense that the mountains, the nearest 15 miles away, look close enough to reach out & touch.
... Humpbacked whales ...
Tuesday 21st December
Anvers Island,
Brabant Island & Antarctic Peninsula

In the evening I decided that tea would definitely not be enough and headed for the gin cupboard where I poured myself a large double and took it back to my cabin with two cans of tonic. Tomorrow morning we head down the narrow and spectacular Lemaire Channel, favourite of cruise ships so nicknamed 'Kodak Alley'. The mood on board is buoyant!

Wednesday 22nd December: *I was up at 7.30 hoping to make the most of today's scenery, but it was snowing and visibility was poor. I sketched the officers on the Bridge who were concentrating hard on steering, making continuous course alterations to avoid the bigger 'growlers' scattered amongst the flat sea ice. As we approached Lemaire Channel, the sea ice gradually thickened and although the visibility didn't improve, the channel is so steep sided and narrow that we could see walls of ice and rock either side of us disappearing into the clouds and mist.*

The muffled silence was broken only by the scrunching of ice floes as the bow shoved through them – and for a while, until they ran out of snow, the yells and laughter of the ship's company having a snowball fight between bridge roof and foredeck. Wildlife was dwarfed by the scale of the landscape – a small group of gentoo penguins on an ice floe, several solitary Weddell seals waking up and realising that there was a ship bearing down on them, shuffling off their ice bed as it was shoved aside by the bow.

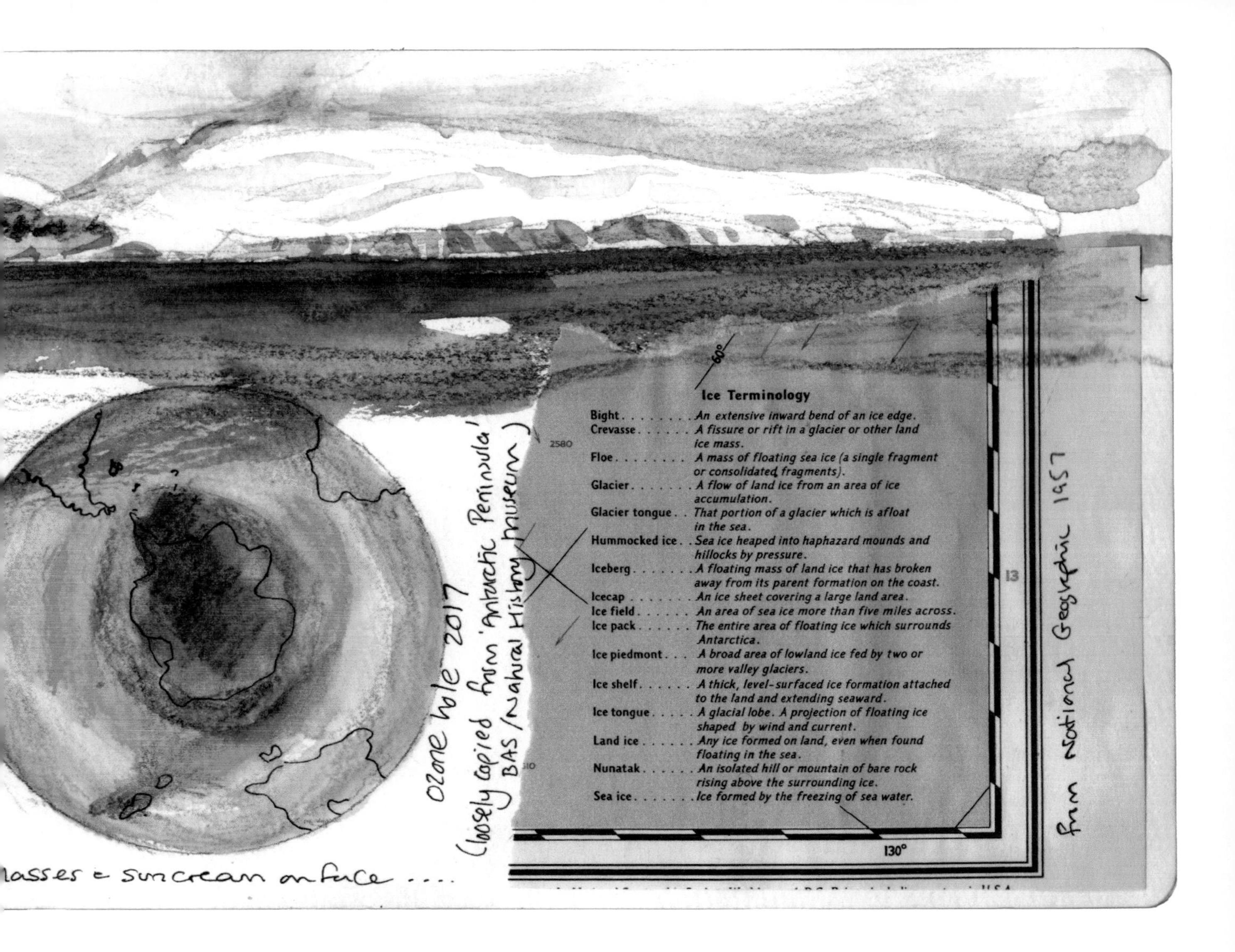

Ice Terminology
Bight. . . . . . . .An extensive inward bend of an ice edge.
Crevasse. . . . . . A fissure or rift in a glacier or other land ice mass.
Floe. . . . . A mass of floating sea ice (a single fragment or consolidated fragments).
Glacier. . . . . . . A flow of land ice from an area of ice accumulation.
Glacier tongue. . That portion of a glacier which is afloat in the sea.
Hummocked ice. . Sea ice heaped into haphazard mounds and hillocks by pressure.
Iceberg. . . . . . .A floating mass of land ice that has broken away from its parent formation on the coast.
Icecap . . . . An ice sheet covering a large land area.
Ice field. . . . . . An area of sea ice more than five miles across.
Ice pack. . . . . . The entire area of floating ice which surrounds Antarctica.
Ice piedmont. . . A broad area of lowland ice fed by two or more valley glaciers.
Ice shelf. . . . . . A thick, level-surfaced ice formation attached to the land and extending seaward.
Ice tongue. . . . . A glacial lobe. A projection of floating ice shaped by wind and current.
Land ice . . . . . . Any ice formed on land, even when found floating in the sea.
Nunatak. . . . . . An isolated hill or mountain of bare rock rising above the surrounding ice.
Sea ice. . . . . . . Ice formed by the freezing of sea water.
130°
Ozone hole 2017
(loosely copied from 'Antarctic Peninsula' BAS / Natural History Museum)
from National Geographic 1957
lasses & suncream on face ...

By the time we were through the Channel, there was nothing to see but white. White sea and white sky, snow still falling.

Today my thoughts turned to how sailors' routine has changed over the centuries. Ships without sails don't keep their crew fit, so they need a gym and a fitness instructor. Most tasks revolve around a computer screen, apart from handling lines and other deck jobs which haven't changed much. Even lowering the boats over the side is a sitting down job for the cranesman. Boats of course have outboards or inboards, nobody rows unless they have to.

Recreation mainly involves a screen too. Apart from intense games of uckers, a complicated board game with a passing resemblance to ludo, most of the time the officers in the wardroom are watching films or playing computer games on the large TV screen. In the past, off watch sailors obviously played games too, but they also created things – scrimshaw, decorative knotwork, paintings of ships on their sea chests. Nobody gets bored enough to be creative now; none of HMS Protector*'s crew would sit in the wardroom painting or making carrick mats. There is little music too. Although there is a guitar in the wardroom and occasionally someone strums a few chords, nobody sings.*

'Computers don't sing shanties
Work is done by microchip
No need for songs or stories
On a modern cargo ship
No need to beat a rhythm
When you're working a machine
Now all your songs and stories
Come from a TV screen

You could say that things are better
For a sailor's life was hard
And a heated cabin's nicer
Than a freezing topsail yard
But you never get to see the world
For harbour time is short
There's no time to find a bar
Or a girl in every port'

On my last visit to the museum in Stanley I was fascinated by the samples of sailor's painted sea chests, many of which were elaborately decorated in the inside of the lids as well as the outside. So this was done purely for their own pleasure rather than to impress others. When did art become something that only 'artists' do?

DECORATED LID FROM A SEAMAN'S CHEST. Sailors frequently painted portraits of their favourite ships on the inside of their chest lids.

TUESDAY 21ST DECEMBER Near Anvers & Brabant Island. Sunny & clear

keep fit circuits take place on deck instead of in the hold

("Are you cold?" "No!" "Keep moving!")

Into Lemaire Strait.
Deep silence except for
engines hum & sea ice
crunching as we push through
Starboard 30 235 midships
Port 20

WEDNESDAY 22nd DECEMBER

8.30. Passage through the Lemaire Strait in snow and poor visibility.

Ice increases to 10/10 cover as we go through the Strait.

gentoos on an ice floe

patterns in the ice, shades & shapes of white & blue

Weddell seals look
bemused when their ice
floe is shoved aside
View from the Bridge deck 1130
Sunglasses needed
still snowing

LEMAIRE CHANNEL
225
.635
LEMAIRE CHANNEL
BOOTH ISLAND
Loubat Pt.
.1174
276
Deloncie
Bay

contents of the huts just as they were left in 1960. workshop, bunks, mangle, storerooms.

(everything was tin, wood, paper - no plastic that I could see)

Huts on Horseshoe Island. Established in 1955

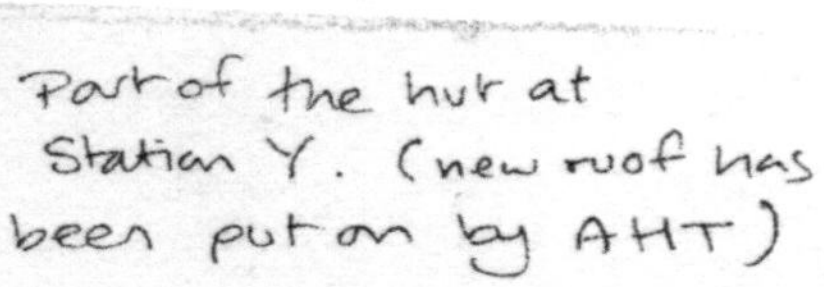

Part of the hut at Station Y. (new roof has been put on by AHT)

67° 48'S 67° 18'W

22nd December

HORSESHOE ISLAND

'Station Y' was established here until 1960. The huts are all still as they were left. Now a UKAHT site.

* "Research here included topographical survey, geology and meteorology. The buildings and artefacts remain virtually unaltered and are in good condition, offering a representation of the scientific research station prior to its closure." (AHT)

23rd December   Horseshoe Island

Ice all around, snowing heavily

All is white & blue except for seal on an ice floe

23rd December. Horseshoe Island. Overcast, snowing.

24th December Ship is surveying, amongst ice, rock & sky

Exploring patterns & shapes of ice & rock

24th December 2021
Antarctica is a feeling

· SKY · ROCK · SILENCE ·

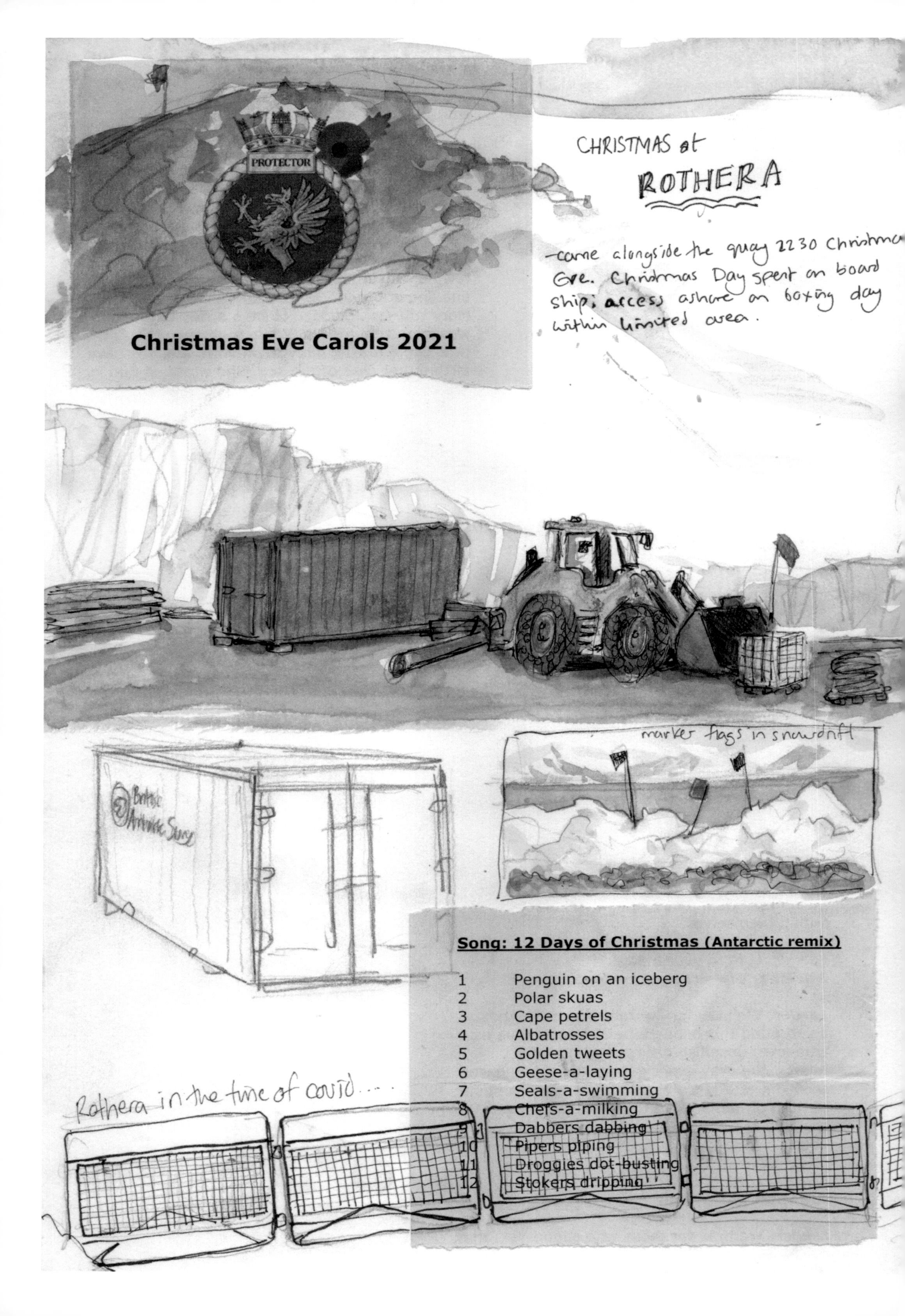
PROTECTOR
Christmas Eve Carols 2021
CHRISTMAS at
ROTHERA
-came alongside the quay 2230 Christmas Eve. Christmas Day spent on board ship; access ashore on boxing day within limited area.
marker flags in snowdrift
Song: 12 Days of Christmas (Antarctic remix)
1 Penguin on an iceberg
2 Polar skuas
3 Cape petrels
4 Albatrosses
5 Golden tweets
6 Geese-a-laying
7 Seals-a-swimming
8 Chefs-a-milking
9 Dabbers dabbing
10 Pipers piping
11 Droggies dot-busting
12 Stokers dripping
Rothera in the time of covid...

Seashell (limpet) found in the
snow at the side of the
runway

Thursday 23rd December: *Icebergs surround us and close by is a black snow patched island with a couple of small huts visible. This is Horseshoe Island, home of Station Y, built in 1955. It's now an Antarctic Heritage Trust site and I was looking forward to seeing the huts which had been left exactly as they were when the site was abandoned in 1960. Whilst on deck I managed a bit of frantic blue pencil sketching on deck as the snow fell onto the paper.*

Shore parties were announced with the first stick at 11 – so that was me, and I managed to nab the extra small survival suit this time. Landing was tricky with the RIB trying to hold its bow against a rock in spite of lumps of ice and a small swell, but we all jumped safely ashore, climbed out of our survival suits and into our shore gear for the walk to the huts. This was part rock scramble, part deep snow. The air was still, snow was falling gently and our exertion kept us warm. I didn't even need gloves. We paused on the walk to watch a group of Adélie penguins tobogganing. Yes – really! Two of them waddled uphill, lay on their stomachs and, after a quick push with their stubby wings, slid down the slope. One standing at the bottom watched and then hurried up the slope to give it a try.

There was no time to sketch. By the time we had walked to the hut and had a quick look round inside, it was time to hurry back to the meeting place. I created my sketchbook pages from a few photos and views from the ship. The hut, Station Y, was a British meteorological research base from 1955 to 1960. It looks much the same inside as it did then, tins on the shelves and the formica table and two chairs, as if the occupants had just gone out for a walk. This site, along with others, is now in the care of the Antarctic Heritage Trust and the purpose of our visit was to check the state of the roof which had been repaired after storms.

Friday 24th December: *It is still overcast with occasional snow, so although it would be good to see the sun – and the colours would be astonishing – this weather suits the landscape of high mountains, the snowfall slumped in wedges down the sides and at the bottom of the steep slopes. I've been trying to work out the patterns and shapes of the exposed rocks between each frozen fall of snow. After a day surveying, we're waiting to go into the BAS base at Rothera. The crew are keen to come alongside and down tools for Christmas, but we have to wait for the day's flights to finish as our mooring is at the end of the airstrip.*

I enjoyed sketching in the light snowfall, there's something magical about the big flakes landing on my sketchbook and creating random effects with my paint or watercolour pencils. I have to stop when the paper gets too wet as I'm using my big hand-made sketchbook with cartridge paper that buckles easily. I keep popping in and out all day – outside to sketch, inside to let the paper dry, then outside again to see where we are and what to draw, then inside to finish off all the half finished scribbles. I've decided to glue two pages together for the rest of the book, to give each page a bit more strength if it gets soggy.

Yes it's cold – but not uncomfortably cold. I was puzzling about this up on the bridge deck just now and Paul, the ship's navigator, explained that it's dry cold, which makes a big difference. At home cold weather makes me feel stressed and grumpy, very much 'in retreat'. My friends laughed when I said I was coming to Antarctica – 'you'll never cope!' they said. But the cold here just makes me feel awake and alive. I'm also getting better at judging what to wear for a spell on deck, and the gear I brought is more than up to it.

I'm trying to work out what makes Antarctica feel so special. This is the best I can do so far:

Whatever it is – that muzziness, blurring of the senses, background noise – that usually stops you feeling that you're completely alive, is gone. There is nothing between you and your experience. Everything looks closer, more real, more intense. The smell of air, salt and ice makes your senses tingle. It's as if the atmosphere is thinner – perhaps it is – but each breath you take feels like you've not been breathing properly for years. It's not just about what it looks like, because photos don't capture it; it's what it feels like, what it does to you, as if you've been asleep all your life and suddenly woken up refreshed. There are places like this all over the world – I've had a taste of it at sea – and there are other ways to reach this clarity, but here you're immersed in it as soon as you step out on deck and take a breath.

We finally berthed alongside the quay at British Antarctic Survey Rothera base at about 2230. It was still daylight, of course. At 2330 it was midnight mass in the conference room. I thought I'd turn up to support the Bish and there was only me, Amy with her flute, the captain and the commander. Earlier, at 1930, we had a carol service in the hold but that was strange – only eight of us there, belting out carols amongst the containers, fighting the engine noise by singing along to a very loud soundtrack.

Once we were alongside the quay, the crew got very quickly into party mode. I was in my cabin after the midnight mass when Michael popped his head round my door and asked if I wanted to join them in the wardroom. I had a couple of glasses then bowed out at 0200.

25th December: *We're alongside, but not able to go ashore until tomorrow. Most of the ship's company were happy to have a proper day off. I'm not surprised – this is the first time the ship has been alongside a quay since South Georgia; so for most of the last month she has been under way, with a full watch on duty. Phoebe and Kasey knocked on my door mid morning and invited me down to the junior mess for a drink. The room was humming like a disco with flashing Christmas lights and a party atmosphere – my entry dramatically increased the average age. A bottle of something blue and vodka-tasting was put into my hand.*

I was on the first sitting for Christmas dinner, a hectic affair in which the tradition is that the officers cook the meal and then serve the rest of the crew. Plates were piled high with all the trimmings – mine was a nut roast made by Kasey. There was a quick swap around for the second sitting. I was told that as a guest I didn't have to help serve but of course I did join in, made myself useful taking platefuls to tables and dodging flying sprouts. When I carried a pile of plates into the washing up area I came across the Captain with a mop and bucket cleaning the galley floor. The noise levels increased with the amount of wine drunk.

I felt restless in the afternoon, thinking of the things I would usually do on Christmas day – go for a walk, get together with friends. We're not able to go ashore until tomorrow so there's no way of walking off the Christmas dinner! At least wifi was working reasonably well today and I had the chance to make a phone call home. Being three hours behind meant that social media went quiet by 0900 because everyone at home was asleep by midnight.

It's not unusual to have Christmas away. I thought back to the Christmas before last, spent close to Cape Horn on sailing ship Tecla *and that didn't feel so strange, surprisingly – I think because we had plenty to keep us busy with the sailing of the ship. I reminded myself that being a long way from home is what I spend much of my time planning and looking forward to!*

Sunday 26th December: *The homesick blues were banished today by the first deep breath of Antarctic air on a walk ashore, and a return to the pleasure of sketching. The staff at the British Antarctic Survey station were keeping to strict social distancing rules but we had access to most of the airfield to go for a walk. Many of the crew set about jogging round it, including the Bish who was running a marathon for charity dressed in a penguin suit and spent most of the day going round and round until he'd clocked up enough miles. He limped back to the ship just in time for supper which I brought up for him as he was too exhausted to go down to the dining room.*

In spite of the limited access, there was plenty to keep me happy sketching. I wished it was possible to visit the base properly, talk to the people who worked here and go tobogganing on the fabulous hill opposite the airstrip where I could see a few people skiing. It's no use, I'll just have to find a way to get back here another time. I had a bit of luck when sketching right at the end of the airstrip where a line of barrels marked the limit of our permitted access. A man holding a snowboard walked past me as I sketched; he was heading for the snowy hill and stopped to chat, at an appropriate distance. Pete Hill is a sculptor, working for BAS as a boatman for his 'day job'. We chatted boats and art and I'll look him up when I get home as he and his sister Sue created some sculptures for Heligan gardens in Cornwall. Fancy meeting two sculptors on my trip!

Wednesday 29th December: *The sun shone today for a spectacular return through the Lemaire Channel. We were out at sea this morning, well offshore and heading north outside the islands. By lunchtime we were heading back into the ice. I took up position on the foredeck, fascinated by the sounds, by the shapes and colours and by the occasional penguins and seals whose peace and occasionally ice floe was shattered by our passing. The seals' attitude was to stay put, brazen it out and act as if we weren't there at all, even when our bow was inches away from them. The penguins were more fearful, scattering frantically even when we were several ice-floes away. The weather became warm as we entered the sheltered waters of the channel, which from a distance looked impossibly narrow and iced up; the scrunching from the bow became more spectacular as the channel narrowed. This time we could see the tops of the mountains that rise almost vertically from the sea – and plunge 200 metres below the surface.*

Monday
27th December.

planned hut inspection on Blaiklock Island cancelled due to too much sea ice for the rib.

gap in the clouds – a sudden glimpse of snow
covered mountains . Look up!

27th December ~ impressions on the move, ice, sky & rock as the ship surveys around Pourquoi Pas Island. Sunshine & snow showers

27th December
Bourgeois Fjord

Tuesday 28th December

Icebergs & sea ice on the way to San Martin (68°S)

"He fell in with great Islands of Ice, of Soe Incredible a hight and Magnitude that I scarce dare to write my thoughts of it" (Edmund Halley, 1 February 1700 at latitude 52° 24'S)

Icebergs more than 10 nm across are given an ID letter & number by US National Ice Center and are tracked by satellite until they shrink below this size.

Wednesday 29th December
Sounds ... of crunching ice, popping e
crackling, crumbling slush
and splitting ice floes
as one rides over another.
Smells ... the intense clarity
of a warm spring day
by the sea.

Approaching Lemaire Channel

LEMAIRE CHANNEL ... 1000 metres above sea level, over 200 metres deep.
the ship moving slowly, threading her way
between the bigger lumps of ice,
crunching through the rest.

Wednesday 29th December
Gentoos' reaction to the approaching ship ...
run away! run away!

weddell seal
The seal's response:-
'move off this comfortable
ice floe? I don't think so!'

on the foredeck
patterns in the ice

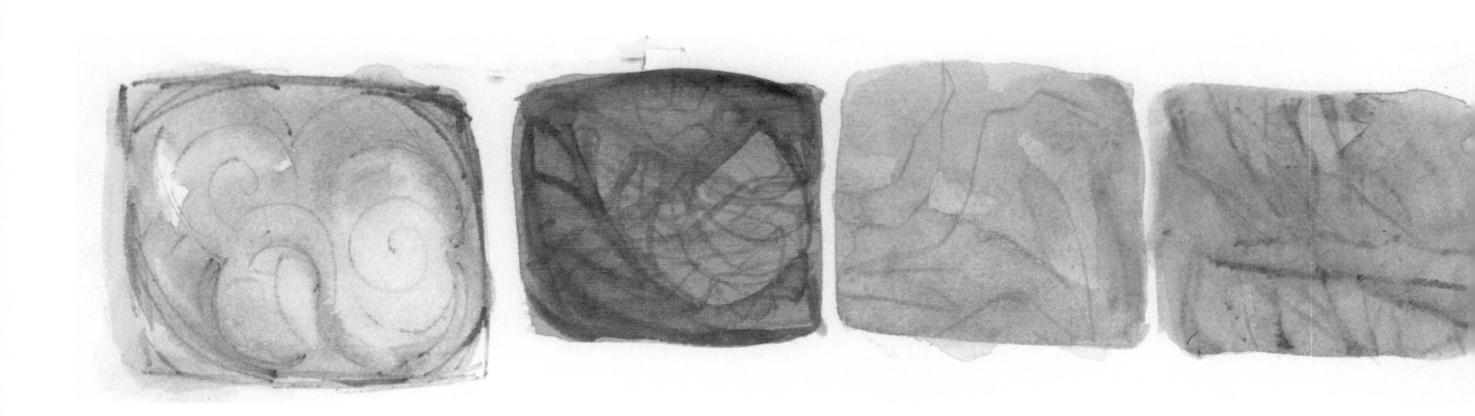

Cabin doodles

ISLAND OF ICE AND FIRE

Friday 31st December
Leaving Deception Island, 1330
40 knots of wind. Didn't make it ashore
as wind increased after first shore party
came back.
"The last day of the old year: May the
new one bring us good fortune, a
safe deliverance from this anxious
time and all good things to those we
love so far away" (Shackleton)

'Last day of the old year: may the new one bring us good fortune, a safe deliverance from this anxious time and all good things to those we love so far away.'

(Ernest Shackleton)

Whalers and sealers ventured ever further south as their prey became harder to find. Deception Island lies between the South Shetland Islands and the tip of Antarctic Peninsula and it was our final stop before returning to the Falklands. It's the only volcano of this island chain that is still active; the last eruption was in 1991, damaging two research stations. The island was named by American sealer Nathaniel Palmer, who thought it was a completely circular island until he discovered the narrow entrance into the caldera at the centre of this volcano. The enclosed bay offered a perfectly sheltered anchorage once the ships had managed to battle through the windy narrows, named Neptune's Bellows. I was glad of HMS *Protector*'s powerful engines as we punched through the funnelling wind into the wider bay of the caldera.

It was hard to imagine how anyone could live here at all, but between 1912 and the 1930s there were up to 150 people working on this remote rock of ash and ice. When the whalers left, several countries showed an interest in the island, but activity from the island's live volcanos meant that it was once again abandoned. Now the scientists are back, along with the tourists. Deception Island has it all – ice, volcanoes, dramatic scenery, an abandoned whaling station and even warm sea water in places due to molten rock below the surface. We weren't given the opportunity for a dip!

Thursday 30th December: *This evening we arrived at Deception island. The approach was spectacular with low sunlight over the cliffs and an icy wind as the ship punched through Neptune's Bellows into the sheltered bay of the caldera, a monochrome landscape of black rock and white snow. I managed a couple of very scribbly sketches from the bridge roof as we approached – goodness, that wind could strip the skin from your face! Inside the entrance was a five mile wide bay, black hills streaked with snow all around. There are the remains of a whaling station at Whalers Bay, and a small cruise ship was anchored off. The plan is to go ashore tomorrow morning.*

Friday
30th December
Approaching Deception Island. 1930
entrance to the
caldera is called
Neptune's Bellows.
Very very windy!

'The only active volcano in the Antarctic Peninsula region'
~~ sketching in the wind ~~ on the bridge roof ~~
Black rock + volcanic dust, white snow
Eastern edge of island

Friday 31st December. Leaving Deception Island, 1330
40 knots of wind. Didn't make it ashore
as wind increased after first shore party
came back.
Port Foster
Craters
Old whaling
station
Whalers
Bay
Neptune's
Bellows
63°S
lagoon is 8km
(5 miles) wide
DECEPTION
ISLAND
60° 30' W

"The last day of the old year: May the new one bring us good fortune, a safe deliverance from this anxious time and all good things to those we love so far away" (Shackleton)

The old whaling station – sketched through a lense!

Saturday 31st December: *I was up early, waiting to find out what time the shore parties were starting – I was on stick two. The first one went ok and we all got suited up ready for the second, but at the last minute it was cancelled as the wind was becoming too strong. Such a shame! The crew of the cruise ship nearby were struggling to get their passengers back on board in a smother of spray. I tried to photograph the view of the old whaling station with my zoom lens so that I could at least do a sketch from that. The structures looked very similar to those on South Georgia only a great deal more derelict, set against the bleak background of the black earth and ash-stained snow.*

By mid evening we were back at sea. Plans for an overnight stay and New Year's Eve celebrations were cancelled as there is rough weather coming and the Captain needs to get ahead of it and head for the Falklands. We came out of Neptune's Bellows into a wild sea, shot with indigo and gold in the twilight. I thought it might be too rough for any kind of socialising but Michael knocked and asked if I wanted to join him for a drink, so that was a pleasant hour or so in his cabin talking about life, birds, ships and Navy life.

Saturday 1st January: *The sea is rough but after a cup of tea and a shower I found I could read, draw, do a few things as long as I stopped to rest my eyes regularly. I skipped lunch and spend a quiet afternoon in the cabin, with a brief outing to sketch the sea. All of the deck areas are off limits because of the weather apart from the vaping area which is conveniently sheltered and close to my cabin. Sleep was intermittent as the ship was butting into a rough sea so the motion was jerky and erratic, throwing me around in the bunk.*

I had more thoughts during the night on what Antarctica feels like. Normal life is like looking through a window – you can see it, engage with it but not quite be wholly in it. Sometimes the window is dirty, sometimes you feel even more removed and 'inside'. Going south is like opening the window and breathing fresh air for the first time. You can reach out and touch life, or at least you feel as though you can. That's why the photos don't work very well; they put you back inside and the mountains that touch the sky look like nothing very much. Most of the time, photos diminish landscapes, like bringing a wild animal indoors and taming it. Photos work best for close ups, perfect for wildlife and for people. Photos put you back behind glass, behind the window again, even though the view is one you won't have seen before.

Sunday 2nd January: *At sea, again quite lively and the decks were out of bounds all day. Luckily I didn't know this the first time I went out, so I was on the main deck for a while, enjoying the sparkle of sunlight on spray, gazing at the sea and birds and doing my sea sketch for a while until a member of crew sent me back indoors!*

Monday 3rd January: *Mid morning and the Falklands are on the horizon. I went on deck with my usual layers on and realised with surprise that it wasn't very cold. There's a kind of melancholy that comes with the end of a voyage, a mourning for – what? Everything I didn't see? Everything I did see but know I'll never see again? It's always a wrench leaving the sea, that special feeling that the deep ocean has, the sharpness and clarity of the air. Already it's changed. Although the sea is still a steel grey outside and there are white caps on the waves, you can smell the land – a 'nearly home' smell. After being away from greenery for several weeks the smell of grass and growing things is striking as we approach the land.*

Tuesday 4th January: *We're back in Mare Harbour and there's an end of term feel to the ship, plenty of cleaning going on and many announcements. I've made a start on gathering up my belongings and tidying the cabin. As the trip went on I've occupied it more and more, filling up the few spare cupboards and drawers, filling the walls with a map of the Antarctic Peninsula and fragments of artwork.*

Thursday 6th January: *I thought these final few days would drag but in fact they've flown by. I had hopes today of going for a walk with Michael but he was busy helping with unloading stores – the hold is open and the crane has been busy all morning as vans arrive on the quay with pallets of stuff. Some of it was unpacked very quickly too – there was fresh cucumber and lettuce for supper! I think I never want to see chips and beans again as long as I live.*

Amongst all the busyness of hard hats, cranes and containers, the Captain found time to address the ship's company as we stood in ranks on the quayside. I'm grateful now that I know the 'stand at ease' stance. There were echoes of past captains in his words as he thanked everyone for their part in making the voyage successful, every task fulfilled, many more miles of ocean surveyed. Soon the ship would be heading south again. I didn't want to leave, I wanted to go with them.

But it was time to go home.

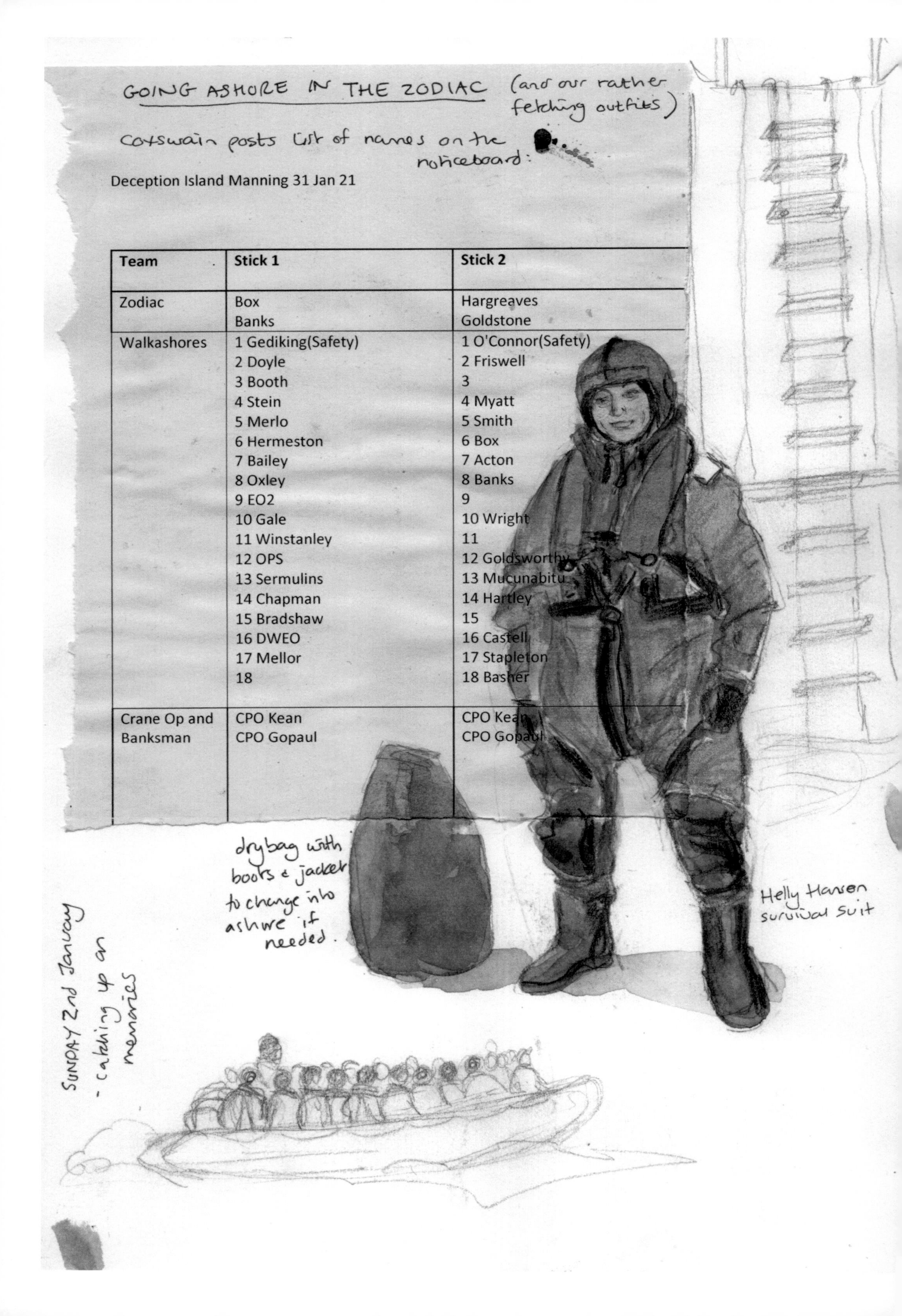

GOING ASHORE IN THE ZODIAC (and our rather fetching outfits)
Coxswain posts list of names on the noticeboard:
drybag with boots & jacket to change into ashore if needed.
Helly Hansen survival suit
SUNDAY 2nd January - catching up on memories

Deception Island Manning 31 Jan 21

Team	Stick 1	Stick 2
Zodiac	Box Banks	Hargreaves Goldstone
Walkashores	1 Gediking(Safety) 2 Doyle 3 Booth 4 Stein 5 Merlo 6 Hermeston 7 Bailey 8 Oxley 9 EO2 10 Gale 11 Winstanley 12 OPS 13 Sermulins 14 Chapman 15 Bradshaw 16 DWEO 17 Mellor 18	1 O'Connor(Safety) 2 Friswell 3 4 Myatt 5 Smith 6 Box 7 Acton 8 Banks 9 10 Wright 11 12 Goldsworthy 13 Mucunabitu 14 Hartley 15 16 Castell 17 Stapleton 18 Basher
Crane Op and Banksman	CPO Kean CPO Gopaul	CPO Kean CPO Gopaul

Amy playing for the hymns -
Sunday service in the Conference Room
1330
O, hear us when we cry to thee,
for those in peril on the sea.

Rough sea so decks are
off limits. Catching up on
sketches from photos.
Skipped lunch, went to church!

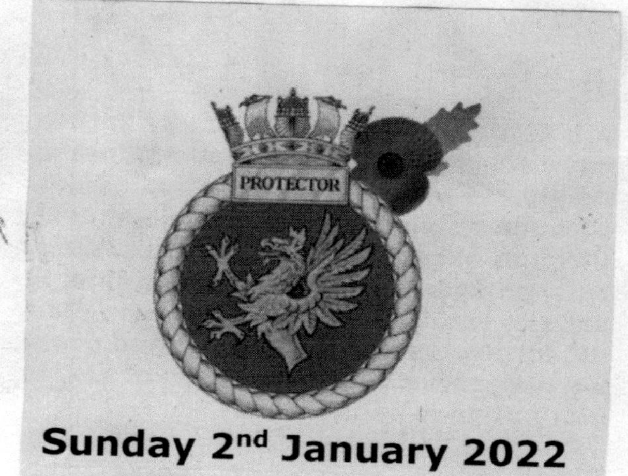

MARE HARBOUR, FALKLANDS   Birds by the ship   Tuesday 4th January

ROCK SHAG AFLOAT – hard to see where feathers end and water begins.

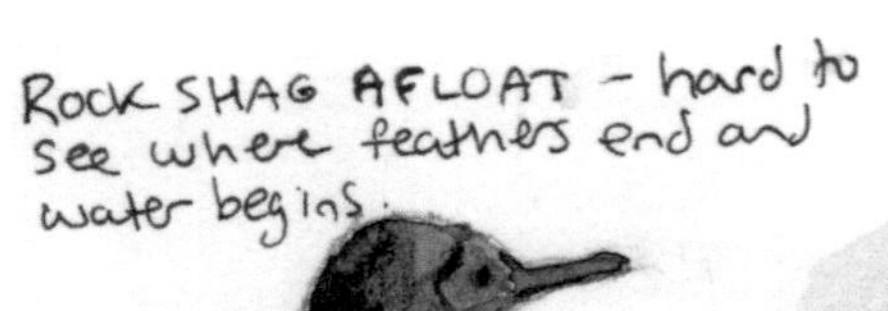

on the quayside

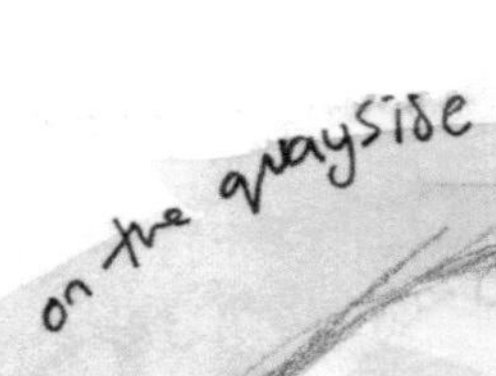

KELP GULL

under the jetty

BLACK-CROWNED NIGHT HERON

on the quayside

SNOWY SHEATHBILL

ROCK SHAGS

on the ledge under the jetty, parents & chicks

BLACK-BROWED ALBATROSS

Riding the wind above the ship

"stand by for take-off!"

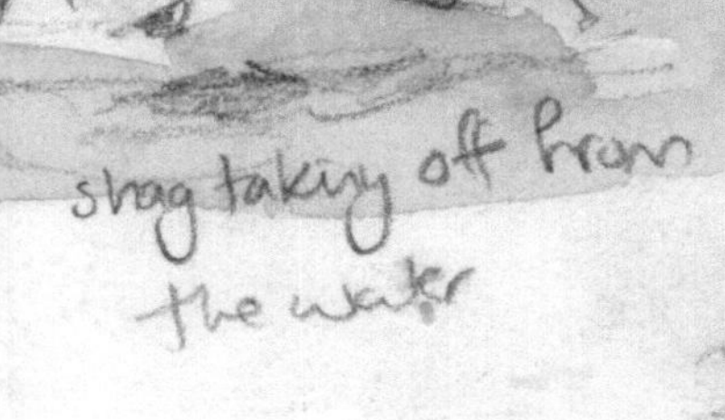

shag taking off from the water

FALKLANDS STEAMER DUCK & CHICKS

KELP GOOSE

Thursday 6th January

Last day on board HMS Protector.

Captain gives an end-of-tour speech to all the crew

would like to go to Antarctica all over again – I feel as if I'm starting to get the hang of this sketching lark!

And I have some blank pages left ....

5th January - very quick ride to Stanley in the morning. Time for the fastest visit ever to the museum to grab a few photos.

(Last time I was at the museum I had plenty of time & no camera so spent the time sketching. This time the sketching has to be from photos - wish I'd taken more of the gentoo!)

bottom part of beak - missing? or not made of bone? check

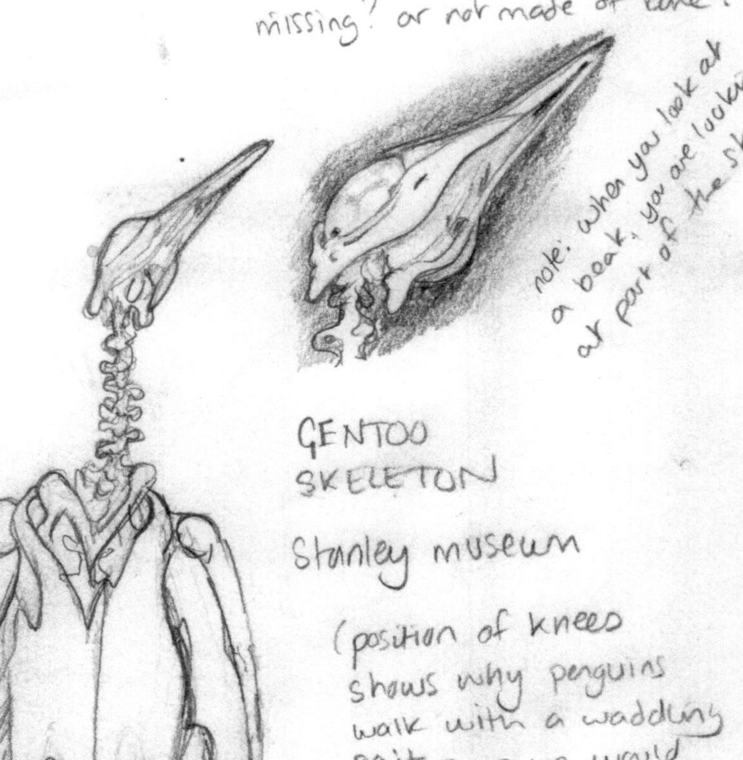

Stanley museum

(position of knees shows why penguins walk with a waddling gait - as we would do if we walked whilst squatting)

(Very sharp teeth! Glad I was able to run faster than the one who came at me in South Georgia)

- can open jaw very wide

Saturday 1st January 2022

moderate to rough sea, heading north to Falklands

THE SOUTHERN OCEAN

Every day at sea I went on deck and sketched the sea in a small sketchbook that folded out, concertina-like, into one long piece of paper. For continuity I drew the horizon in the same place each day. At the end of the voyage I spread the whole 17 page frieze out so that I could see the subtle changes in shape and light from day to day, with the increasing presence of ice as we headed south.

The sea is so much more than the wet bit between the dry bits. Each ocean has a presence and a character of its own. This was my second visit to the Southern Ocean and I love its fierce beauty, the shift in colours from steel grey to liquid sapphire, the bright snow petrels and prions dancing in the bow wave. 'But isn't it really rough down there?' my friends ask. Well, yes it can be, but if you're in those waters you're going to be in a ship built to take it. I've been sicker on the brown, lumpy waters of the North Sea than I have down in the far south. At least in the south there is always an albatross soaring astern, swooping to clip the wave crests and lifting the spirits by the perfection of those knife-like wings.

The Southern Ocean circles Antarctica and was only recently officially recognised by National Geographic cartographers as an ocean in its own right. It's far from our lives and far from our thoughts but we depend upon it for our existence. Oceans absorb 93% of the heat produced by global warming. The Southern Ocean is one of the smallest but it takes 75% of that total. The reasons for this lie in its depth, temperature and unique circulation which can enable heat and CO_2 to be exchanged at a deep level. It forms a girdle around Antarctica, a boundary between the icy water south and warmer water north. It also supports a wide range of life – over 9,000 known species.

I am grateful to the scientists who are studying this globally significant area. There is a wealth of information online, especially with the British Antarctic Survey's website.

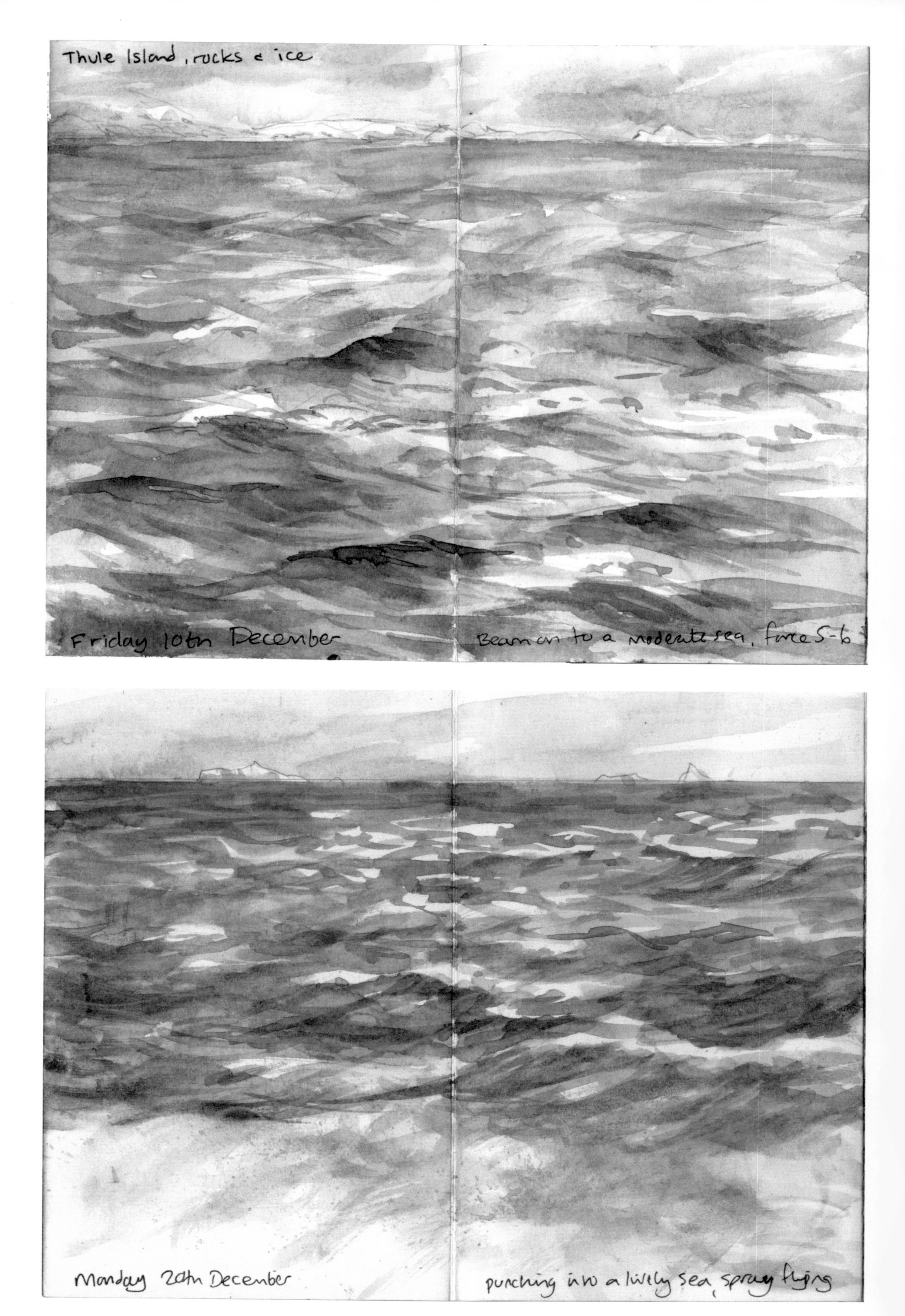
Thule Island, rocks & ice
Friday 10th December
Beam on to a moderate sea, force 5-6
Monday 20th December
punching into a lively sea, spray flying

crossed 60°S latitude today
Monday 13th December
heading into modeate-rough sea

Heading for Lemaire Channel
Wednesday 22nd December

ARTISTS ON THE MOVE

'It is a good test if you can discover something in your sketch which you did not realise when you drew it'

(Edward Wilson)

I like to work from life as often as possible, however difficult the circumstances. In extreme conditions there is no way that a photograph can capture what you are feeling. When snow is falling and blurring the freshly laid paint, fingers are going numb and you only manage a few scribbly marks, those marks will capture something that would never be there if you skipped this stage and waited until you were in a warm room looking at a flat image on a small screen.

The role of the camera

I often travel to new places without a camera. It makes me use my sketchbook more and avoid the 'snap trap' – the habit of reaching for phone or camera simply because you are in front of something new, and because it's easy. Taking a photo sends a message to your brain 'I can look at this properly later'. There are times when that is very useful, but occasionally I like to ignore the urge to take a photo and, whether sketching or not, focus wholly on the experience. My visual memory improves when I know I can't look at it again later; I notice more, work harder at looking.

It's also true that a camera is a huge help to the artist, especially when you are constantly on the move. I took a Lumix pocket camera with me to Antarctica as I knew I would need as much reference material as possible but didn't want to carry too much gear or spend valuable sketching time changing lenses.

With short bursts of time ashore and plenty of time at sea in my cabin, I used a happy mix of photos, memory and imagination to add to my sketches, draw close up studies of penguins and other wildlife, experiment with ideas and play around with colours. During our voyage south, I could hear the echoes of sailors down the centuries, explorers, whalers and sealers, their ships and their lives so different from my own. Other past echoes came from the artists who travelled with the explorers; how similar the sights they picked up their pencils to draw, but how different the circumstances.

Before the age of the camera, an artist's task was very different to my own free and easy sketchbooks. A ship's artist accompanying an expedition had to be the camera; his sketches were the only way that people back home were going to see what he had seen; the only way that naturalists and scientists could identify and catalogue new species. He had to be an expert at killing and preparing his subjects so that he could lay a bird out on the table to draw, spread its wings to study flight feathers, details of beaks or feet that can show the tiny differences between sub-species.

Accessible cameras have changed everything for the artist. We no longer have to kill wildlife to draw it in detail. Photographs have largely replaced drawings as reference for the naturalist; sketchbooks can now be filled in any way and for any reasons the artist chooses.

It is hard to imagine just how much impact our century's avalanche of images has upon our lives and our thinking. A click of the mouse or a glance at social media floods our eyes and minds with photographs of everything we've never seen, from the mundane to the extraordinary. We no longer need to wonder what Antarctica looks like – we've seen the photos. We've seen everything in the world from our sofa. Does this over-exposure dull our senses, so that nothing can surprise us any more? This is another reason to put the camera down, so that I am not always putting an electronic gadget between my eye and my experience.

Sketching brings you back to the present. To draw, you have to look with an intensity that increases the awareness of not just what you are seeing but feelings and impressions too. This happens whether your drawing is 'good' or 'bad'. Drawing is like writing – it's an alphabet of marks that we use to enhance our lives and make it more interesting; we write (and draw) to understand, to communicate and connect. Getting 'better' at it is something that happens along the way.

Edward Wilson (1872–1912)

One of the best known artists from the days of polar exploration was Edward Wilson. He was a doctor and a naturalist with a particular interest in birds, as well as a meticulous artist. He accompanied Scott on the Discovery and Terra Nova expeditions and his detailed notes, paintings and specimens made a huge contribution to the scanty knowledge about Antarctic wildlife.

To draw a moving subject you need a good visual memory, the ability to take a mental photograph of a bird in flight at a particular moment. Then you hold the image in your mind long enough to draw the shapes. Then you do the same again and again for all the variety of shapes that the bird will make, looking for repetition in the cycle of each wing beat to reinforce your observations.

I move fast when sketching birds in flight, making scribbly marks all over the page to try and capture a partial record of the curve of a wing, the shape of the body. I daren't take my eyes off the subject long enough to look at the paper, so the result is a mess of bird-like marks, as you'll have seen from my sketchbook pages. Wilson's bird studies, even the simple outlines, are done with care, so I copied this pencil sketch of a storm petrel as I was interested to know how long a small drawing might take him. It took me 20 minutes and does not have the careful tonal variation that Wilson's sketch had, but I had to slow my pencil down and make small strokes of the pencil. I would not be able to work to this kind of accuracy without a photograph.

His sketches have the discipline born of necessity and show a combination of scientific and artistic integrity, but they also have a lyrical quality that goes beyond the functional.

'Accuracy rather than the making of pictures should be our aim in Antarctica, especially as our sketches are largely concerned with scientific work'

I had reason to be grateful for my little pocket camera when reading Wilson's account of his travels. He complains of the time it takes skinning, cleaning and cataloguing his specimens .... 'a long and tedious job and one which robs me of a lot of time which I would like to devote to working up last summer's sketches....'

The Polar Museum at the Scott Polar Research Institute in Cambridge is home to many of Wilson's sketches and archives.

Sketching on the move – materials

Sketching outside is rarely convenient. There's nowhere to sit, water pots fall over on stony ground, wind blows your pages, hands get cold – and there's that little voice in your head telling you to take a photo and work on it in comfort later. But there are ways to keep it simple and it is always worth it, even if you only make a few hasty marks to finish off later. At least in Antarctica there is no member of the public peering over your shoulder saying, too late, 'ooh, are you drawing, can I look?

I'm emphasising sketching rather than painting here, for whilst I do know and admire artists who can create a finished work of art on location, I am not one of them. I work mostly in sketchbooks, only occasionally on loose sheets clipped to a board. My aim is to capture a series of quick impressions rather than working in detail on one scene. I use my sketchbook as a visual diary, a way of seeing more.

Sketchbooks and paper

I took a selection of hardback sketchbooks and some large pads of A4 watercolour paper. I prefer hardback to spiral bound as the book is more permanent – you're not tempted to tear pages out if you don't like them! It also means that they will lie flat when I want to work across two pages, which I often do when trying to draw big places. My A5 *Seawhite Watercolour Travel Journal* was landscape format which I like, and contained quite heavy paper that took watercolours well.

My A4 sketchbook was hand made by a local bookbinder, a present from a friend. It lay flat beautifully for sketching but contained cartridge paper, normally not a problem for watercolours but it started to buckle when snow fell on it so I started gluing two pages together to strengthen it, which worked well.

I took two 'concertina' style sketchbooks which pull out into one long piece of paper. For the daily sea sketches I used a Moleskine Japanese Album, and another smaller handmade book was perfect for a sequence of ice sketches.

Loose sheets of Saunders Waterford watercolour paper and a few small cartridge paper sketchbooks were also added to the mix.

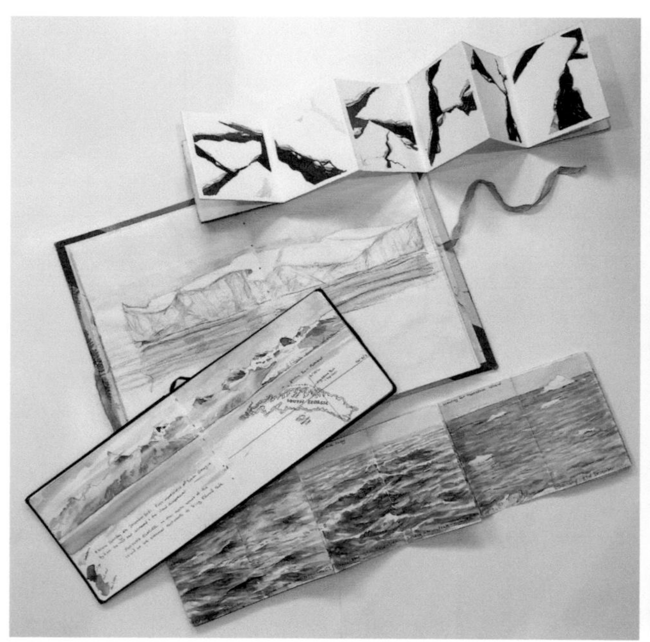

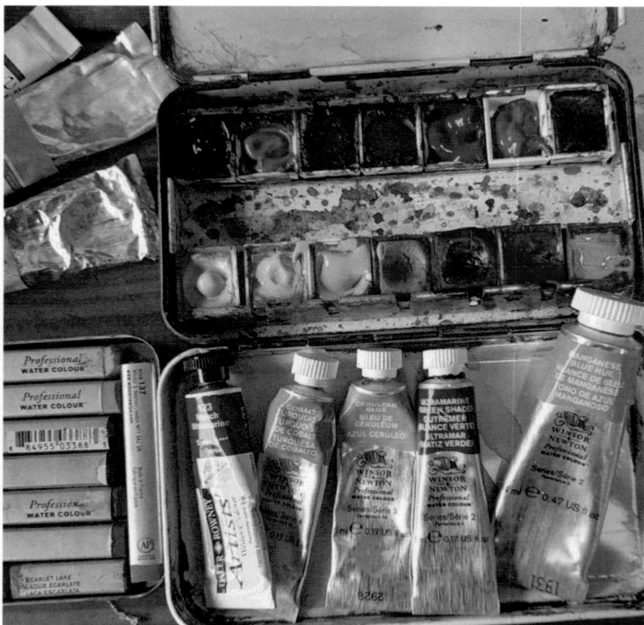

Watercolours

My little box of watercolours has travelled round the world with me, and is perfect for outdoor work. All I need to do is to adjust the colours to fit my destination. Half of the colours are blues anyway, so I just made sure that one of them was turquoise. When the pans run out (quite a few of them did), I top them up from tubes.

Brushes

I took four brushes – three are a set of watercolour travel brushes, and the fourth a Pentel water brush. The water brush as the name suggests has a reservoir of water that you can squeeze into the tip and saves the need for a water pot. This is very useful when working on location, especially if you are standing up and on a moving ship!

Pencils, pens and crayons

I filled a pencil case with as many drawing tools as I could, knowing that I would lose pencils overboard and it's always useful keeping a spare or two in your pocket! As well as assorted pencils and pens, I added a selection of coloured pencils, some of them water soluble and making sure there were plenty of blues.

Water pot

For travelling, I use a small plastic container with a lid, which I fill from a water bottle, or from any convenient source (a stream, snow, the sea). If there's nowhere to put a water pot I'll use the water brush.

I'd been told that in sub-zero temperatures when the water on your brush might freeze, artists use spirits which have a lower freezing point. So I had a miniature bottle of gin with me just in case, but it wasn't cold enough to need it. (I didn't drink it, either!)

Other art materials

- Tracing paper – for tracing maps or transferring images
- Glue stick – for collage, sticking pages together, adding bits and pieces to sketchbooks
- Bulldog clips – to stop pages flapping in the wind

Fingerless gloves

It's so hard to keep hands warm enough when sketching in the cold. Fingerless gloves help but they do affect how you hold your pencil or brush. I found that I ended up taking them off and working really fast to get as much down as possible until my fingers went numb.

RECOMMENDED BOOKS AND WEBSITES

Books

A Great Task of Happiness (the Life of Kathleen Scott), Louisa Young

Terra Incognita, Sara Wheeler (Vintage)

The History of Modern Whaling, J.N. Thonnessen and A.O. Johnsen (Hurst & Co)

Antarctica (Natural History Museum and British Antarctic Survey)

Troubled Waters, Trailing the Albatross, An Artist's Journey, Bruce Pearson (Langford Press)

Birds of the Antarctic, Edward Wilson (edited by Brian Roberts) (New Orchard Editions)

From Pole to Pole: The Life of Quintin Riley 1905-1980, Jonathon Riley (Golden Duck)

The Sea Journal: Seafarers' Sketchbooks, Huw Lewis-Jones (Thames and Hudson)

Websites

Scott Polar Research Institute

www.spri.cam.ac.uk

Join the Friends of SPRI to get involved. There is a polar museum at the Institute HQ in Cambridge with an extensive archive of polar exploration.

British Antarctic Survey

www.bas.ac.uk

Royal Navy and HMS *Protector*

www.royalnavy.mod.uk/our-organisation/the-fighting-arms/surface-fleet/survey/antarctic-patrol-ship/hms-protector

South Georgia Heritage Trust

www.sght.org

South Georgia Museum

www.sgmuseum.gs

UK Antarctic Heritage Trust

www.ukaht.org

Captain Cook's Voyages

www.captaincooksociety.com

Antarctic and Southern Ocean Coalition

www.asoc.org

A short film by Home-Stage.co.uk about my sketchbooks

youtu.be/zWF0iwb2G4s